THE FOURTH ESTATE

A Force Multiplier for the Indian Army

(With the Specific Backdrop of Kargil Battle)

THE FOURTH ESTATE

A Force Multiplier for the Indian Army
(With the Specific Backdrop of Kargil Battle)

Colonel Satish Chandra Tyagi

Established 1870

United Service Institution of India
Admiral R D Katari Chair

GYAN

GYAN PUBLISHING HOUSE
NEW DELHI - 110002

The Fourth Estate

Rs. 540

ISBN : 81-212-0851-3

Published in 2005 in India by
Gyan Publishing House
5- Ansari Road, Daryaganj
New Delhi-110 002
Email : gyanbook@vsnl.com
Visit our Website at : http//www.gyanbooks.com
Phones : 23282060, 23261060, Fax : 23285914

Lasertype Setting by: Tact Computer Graphics, Delhi
Printed at: Mehra Offset Press, Delhi

Contents

Contents

Preface

Being the Commandant of 15 Corps Battle School, I had the opportunity to train some of the battalions which later fought in Kargil and brought glory to the nation. During the Kargil battle, I was assigned the task of compiling an official first hand account of the same. This took me to most of the Posts in Kargil to meet troops and compile their heroic deeds. I was lucky to meet most of them in Mushkoh, Dras, Kaksar, Batalik and Chorbatla. I regret not meeting some of my close associates as they made supreme sacrifice of their lives for the nation. The stories of their brave actions were recorded as a tribute to them and for posterity to remember them.

While in Kargil, I noticed that the media was present in good numbers everywhere. Their spirits and efforts were truly commendable, as some of them wanted to even climb up to Tiger Hill or Tololing with me. For the first time, I realised how much was common between them and us. I also wondered how much effect the media coverage would have back at home or on the front itself! I felt the need for us to understand the media environment as much as I want them to understand the ground realities within the Army. Thus, Kargil became the contemporary platform on which military and media relationship was examined and a case study was done in this research to reach some conclusions to enhance the existing framework.

Although, foreign media was present in Kargil but keeping the Indian perspective in mind, the foreign media was kept outside the confines and scope of this research except the Pakistani media. In the absence of any primary document, research on Pak media is primarily based upon very limited secondary material available. Diplomatic efforts and the political fall-outs too have remained beyond the scope of this research.

I am particularly very grateful to Mr Inder Malhotra, a veteran and an eminent journalist, who consented to be the guide of a soldier who had no prior knowledge of what media really was all about and was embarking upon the temerity to comment upon them. It is to his credit and his worthy guidance that I could proceed ahead. Despite all his commitments, he devoted his very precious time with me whenever I wanted. He encouraged me in channeling my effort and shaping my research work. He has been a great teacher from whom I have learnt a lot.

During the course of the research, the research subject being of a kind that it was, I needed to gather enough nerves and venture into interviewing a large number of leading personalities in different fields. It was very gracious of each one of them to find time for my research and queries. Some of the luminaries who contributed to my research and I am very grateful to are – General VP Malik (Retd), Lieutenant General VR Raghavan (Retd), Lieutenant General YM Bammi (Retd), Lieutenant General VK Kapoor (Retd), Lieutenant General Krishan Pal, Lieutenant General Mohinder Puri, Major General A Chopra, Brigadier CP Khanduri (Retd), Brigadier GL Sachdeva (Retd), Air Commodore Jasjit Singh (Retd), Brigadier SP Sinha (Retd), Brigadier Amar Aul, Brigadier Devinder Singh, Colonel Ajai Shukla (Retd), Colonel R Dargan (Retd), Lieutenent Colonel BK Sharma, Mr G Parthasarthy, Mr BG Verghese, Mr Keith Flory, Mr Praveen Swami, Mr R Prasannan, Mr BM Chengappa, Mr Ajai K Rai, Professor Matin Zuberi, Professor Devendra Kaushik, Dr Raj Kumar, Dr Som Nath Mishra, and Ms Sangeeta Saxena. There are more, whose names do not occur here, which by no means diminishes their graciousness.

I am really thankful to the United Service Institution (USI) to grant me the fullest opportunity to carry out a research on the topic of my choice. I must very particularly and specially thank Lieutenant General Satish Nambiar (Retd), Major General YK Gera (Retd) and Colonel VK Singh (Retd) at the USI, who accepted all my requests at odd hours and offered all the possible support at all the times. I am very grateful to Colonel PK Gautam (Retd) who wouldn't ever forget to lead me on to those related articles and books which I wouldn't have been able to look up ever otherwise. Colonel BS Pama, a colleague at USI, came up with best solutions always and deserves my very special thanks. I am also very thankful to the entire staff at the USI including the staff in the Library who willingly and cheerfully cooperated with me at all times.

I also take this opportunity to very specially thank Major General PK Mahajan, GOC, 6 Mtn Div who, being a Kargil veteran, gave me very valuable insights into Kargil operations, which were hard realities and remained unaccounted for considerations in this research until I spoke to him. I thank Brigadier KS Gulia, Dy GOC, 6 Mtn Div, who benefited me with his immense research and military experience and took pains to advise me on many aspects of this research.

I must very specially thank my wife, Poonam, and my daughters, Pallavi and Shailvi, who were ever patient and did not complain while I sat for longer hours than usual at USI being on study leave. They also became first critics of my work, often giving very valuable ideas and inspiring me to continue putting in hard work without deviating from the main goal.

I dedicate this book to all those who made the supreme sacrifice of their lives in Kargil.

S C Tyagi

New Delhi
August 2004

Introduction

"War is fought with the will of the government, competence of the armed forces and the support of the nation"

Carl Von Clausewitz

Operation VIJAY or Kargil, as it is popularly known, is an apt example of this prophetic remark made by Carl Von Clausewitz. The conflict was truly a war of three 'M's – Military, Media and the Motherland. It was seen on television (TV), heard on radio and read in print by millions and it enjoyed the euphoric support of the nation in its entirety. Beaming it live to the drawing rooms of the millions on the small screen had an effect hitherto unknown and unseen in the annals of Indian history. The TV, radio, newspapers, magazines and periodicals splashed and broadcast the latest pictures and stories of war being fought in the frozen and icy Himalayan landscape. The so-called Fourth Estate, in their characteristic fervour and zeal, ensured no aspect of the battle, particularly of human interest, were left untouched. In a short span of time, India went on an upward swing of mood from the initial shock of getting surprised to a victorious country with her honour restored. The Indian Army once again proved its mettle by pushing back Pakistani invaders perched atop Kargil heights.

What were the factors that assisted the Army in achieving this seemingly impossible task? The so called Mount Casino effect[1], where the enemy gained advantage of height as he sat at the top of mountain ridges and peaks with a little hope to dislodge him from there, did initially result in some hard and pessimistic speculations. It was difficult to believe (on both sides of the border!) that the intruders, who were reasonably well entrenched by then, could be packed and sent back home in a hurry. People needed to know as to how it had happened, who were responsible for it, how long it will take to evict the intruders and all that what was the latest on the front. Media filled this gap. Reporters rushed to Kargil and soon the entire country turned/tuned in to their radios, TV sets and newspapers for the real time battle situations. Unlike the previous wars, this conflict became the first one to be watched live on TV and much more. The phenomenal speed with which the information travelled from the front to the masses back home on electronic as well as print media, earned this battle the designation of being India's first media war. Pakistan's media was under developed and the media battle was asymmetric. Mount Casino effect was soon to be converted into cascading effect, with the Indian military and media in the forefront.

What were the effects of this first media war on the masses and on the conduct of military operations and did the media coverage of the events in Kargil ultimately shape the outcome of the conflict or, in other words, what were the contributions of the media in this battle? Was media-military symbiosis synergetic in India? Did media's role assist the Armed Forces during Kargil? If yes, then how can it be replicated or cloned for future conflicts? Answer to some of these basic questions cannot and should not be ignored for the sake of deriving some lessons for future, especially so when Kargil has widely been accepted as the first media war.

Looking back at the history of the reportage of wars, it is clear that the news from the battlefront has always interested mankind. Media has now assumed a status which it had never enjoyed before. Starting as an institutionalised approach to generate awareness and inform masses, media has become an instrument to govern our lives.[2]

It was a messenger who first gave the news from the battlefront in the early days of mankind. The news about victory in the battle of Marathon was conveyed through a messenger who, after conveying the message (in this case), died at the end of his run due to exhaustion. Marathon Race in the Olympics is a commemoration of the same event, and a big event is aptly called a Marathon event.

Not only was news from the front conveyed to people back home, it was a common practice to record minutest of details of the battle for the sake of posterity. People in India may be aware of the practice prevalent among the Rajput warriors who employed hereditary recorders called *Charans.* A quote from one of the Indian Officers' reflections on the war in Europe in the year 1914 - 15 and the Indian Army's part in it may serve as a good example: "*To my mind, it is a thing of great importance to keep a nation's records...It was my opinion that both (the Maharajas of) Jodhpur and Bikaner who have brought their own troops to fight in this world-wide conflict ought to have brought their own Charans who are our hereditary recorders.*"[3] The same officer suggests the best method to report and to keep records at that time, "*Poetry is the best form in which records ought to be kept. It is only through this means that the great deeds of our heroes from the most ancient times have been kept.*"[4]

Thus, ballads about the bravery in the battle were made and sung and were passed on from one generation to the other.[5] Historians were later employed by the rulers to pen it down. One of the earliest accounts of a battle in India is the epic *Mahabharata.* Although, it is regarded as mythology and not a historical account by some researchers, to discard it for that reason would be to not respect its intrinsic value. It represents Indian thinking and values. Sanjay, who was selected for his unbiased views and truthfulness, was to narrate the complete details of the battle that raged between the Kauravas and Pandavas far away in the battlefield of Kurukshetra through his *Divya Chakshu* (Divine Eyesight) to the blind King Dhritrashtra in his palace. He, thus, could possibly be termed as 'India's first war correspondent'. *Mahabharata* is the written account of the battle. Even the sacred Hindu scripture - *Bhagwad Gita* has been written in the form as narrated by Sanjay. A close scrutiny and study of *Mahabharata* would expose to us the nuances of the battle that went on between the two adversaries and till date it remains a great testimony to what the quality of battlefield reporting analyses was all about during the epic period in India. If we were to identify a war correspondent in correspondingly modern India, possibly William Howard Russell's name could be the first one to be cited as he reported upon the first war of Independence in India in 1857.[6] He, incidentally, was also the first war correspondent who reported upon the Crimean War. Interestingly, another of the reporters was none other than Sir Winston Churchill, posted in India in his early days as a British Indian Army Officer. He later went on to report about the Boer War in Africa.

The Egyptians noted for their sacred writings, the hieroglyphics, discovered the properties of Papyrus plant. We must also correlate the 'Bhojpatra' that was used for recording/writing in ancient India. Babylonians and specially Phoenicians were pioneers in the development of calligraphic writings. Block printing started in Europe by the 15th century.

Oxford Gazette needs to be quoted first to look at the evolution of reporting of the news in Europe. It was founded in 1665 as the first publication designed as a newspaper. It was a controlled publication. London Gazette was the first English newspaper published from London and England's first English daily was Daily Courant.[7]

The coverage of the war has now taken an interesting turn with the arrival of the TV showing pictures from the battlefront. The reach of the TV has now phenomenally expanded with the availability of the satellites in space and has made it possible to view near real time coverage of an event. Incidentally, not many of us are aware that India had successfully pioneered in this field by a programme called SITE (Satellite Instructional Television Experiment), in the year 1975-76, covering 2400 villages in six different states. SITE programme was basically meant for developmental education. The success of this programme saw the beginning of a new era in the coverage of an event in 1982 when the Ninth Asian Games opened in New Delhi. Application of the INSAT technology was used for the first time in India for commercial applications. TV became 'Colour' and a national programme started on Doordarshan. NAM and CHOGM coverage by using microwave links for TV transmission brought events closer home further.[8]

The importance of this experiment lay in the fact that many of the international media barons were eyeing the results of this experiment. They wished to replicate it and derive huge commercial benefits from it. Also, the sizeable untapped Indian market was another bait for them. An opportunity arose in the form of Kargil conflict in the summer of 1999. Media coverage of an event took an upward surge almost nearing a deluge. Twenty four-hour channels began churning the battlefield in a hunt for not only the latest stories but a series of stories each eclipsing the previous one thereby arousing public interest and forming opinions. A hitherto unknown place, Kargil became a rallying point for the nation to strongly unite as one and to support the war effort on the battlefront by all means.

Kargil has become a short hand for a powerful collective experience. Its mere mention conjures vivid images; of betrayal, anxiety, anger, sadness, determination, bravery, triumph and euphoria. Kargil became the new symbol of an uncharacteristically determined India.[9] Pictures in the media and the stories of the war in Kargil created new heroes for the nation. Never had there been so much support to the war effort in recent history as was evident during the Kargil conflict. Why did it happen the way it did – did media play a role in it? Do we expect the media to be as supportive as it was during Kargil? Would the part of the media that is controlled and financed by people from outside the country continue to play the ball the way it did during Kargil? Do we expect certain changes in this pattern of reporting; whether good or bad? Are there any safeguards to ensure that the national interest is looked after in future wars/conflicts? Already, there are people who are questioning the definition of national interest because they know that it is difficult to answer. And once it is difficult to define or answer, even their personal interests can always be interpreted or interpolated as the national interests. Should we or should we not guard against such a situation? Should not there be some justifiable policy to bring the guilty, if any, to book? Should not there be checks and balances to prevent someone taking the nation for a ride? We shall make efforts to examine all these elements subsequently.

It is a known fact now that the Government as well as the society recognises the potency of the Fourth Estate, its role and its importance. In any modern society, the public opinion is formed to a great extent by the information available to the masses, whether authentic or otherwise. Opinion of the masses is one of the key instruments that is largely responsible for influencing the public life and the government in a democratic country. Therefore, we may safely presume the potency of the word 'information'. To a very large extent, in the present day environment, this information is made available and passed on through the medium of newspapers, periodicals, radio and TV channels, which we are collectively referring to as the Media or the Fourth Estate here. Today, the images of war, or for that matter peace, can decisively draw the contours of a nation's will or public opinion even before the authorities can confirm or repudiate the authenticity. Therefore, it is all the more essential to critically analyse the role media can play and how best can it be optimised without compromising any of its elemental virtues.

The impact of media on the conduct and outcome of the battle has always been acknowledged by all rationalists and remains an area of contemporary concern. As seen, there have been evolutionary and revolutionary developments in mass communication technology; from telegraph to satellite communication and from print medium to radio and then to television and now to Internet. With ever multiplying opportunities for communication, the media is registering a continuous growth. The result is for all of us to see in the instant and the graphic coverage of the battles. Kargil was the opening wicket and the learning experience for Indian defence correspondents and the media as a whole. If Kargil was a take off platform for the Indian media, the finesse in reporting the war against terrorism in Afghanistan by Indian media later is a testimony to the fact that media reporting of the war has come of age. The Kargil conflict also saw the transformation of media, a principal tool of information, into one of the war winning factors.

We must not forget that media wields tremendous power of information by way of withholding, delaying or denying "access" to information, and choice of priorities, emphasis and texture of military view, incident or statement. In influencing public opinion it has become so powerful that today's media blitz is said to win or lose wars. Most important, here are not the withholding, delaying or denying of information but the selection of priorities, emphasis and texture of military view as presented by the media.[10] Another aspect that is important for military operations to be successful, is the information warfare. We are now a shift away from traditional methods of application of force and means of combat towards neo evolutionary and non-traditional methods including information.[11] The air force fights the air war, the navy fights the enemy on the high seas and the army combats the foe on land – who then will fight the information war?[12] To be able to successfully combat on this fourth front, the media will have to be one of the integrated components of the total war machinery. Fortunately, increasingly, now states as well as non-state political actors are recognising the immense power of information warfare. Whatever be the scale or scope of an ongoing war, information warfare is an essential component thereof. And for information warfare, media is one of the most important tools and, thus, becoming a war-winning factor. The focus of this research is, however, not to highlight the need to combat the enemy information warfare, which is extremely desirable. The main focus is to present a case where the management of the flow of information and integration of all the elements that constitute it, supplement the war efforts on own side and, thus, become a catalyst for victory.

A nation's military security comes from the strength of its armed forces and the media is considered to be the watchdog of the nation itself. Thus, both contribute towards a common cause. By virtue of the demands and nature of its peculiar employment, the army is required to function in border areas; a little away from the people most of the time. The media becomes the main and probably the only link between the people and the army. Therefore, integration and convergence of aims of the army and the media becomes very important. The Fourth Estate is one of the important pillars of a democratic society and the army upholds and provides the desired security to the same society, thus affording an equal status to both these strengths of a nation. Thomas Jefferson had rated the Press as even more important than the army as a defender of democratic principles because it keeps a sharp eye on the military and the government it serves.

The military is hierarchical with great inter and intra pride and loyalties. It is the antithesis of a political democracy – and must be so if it is to be effective. Many things it legitimately does make little sense to civilians who have scant knowledge of military matters.[13] To the contrary, a free Press or media – one of the great virtues and elemental constituents of a democracy – is an institution wherein concentration of power is viewed as a danger. The Press/media is the watchdog over institutions of power be they military, political, economic or social. Its job is to inform the people about the doings of institutions. By its nature, the Press/media is skeptical and intrusive. As a result, there will always be a divergence of interests between the media and the military.[14] Notwithstanding the differences there are quite a few similarities too; both are dedicated to the nation and their respective professions, are idealistic in their approach and are technically proficient in the jobs that they do. Both work under hardships for long hours and do crave for recognition for their work. Another important factor that must be mentioned here is that army men are team players and content with traditional approach while the journalists are independent and tend to be creative in their approach. In their own ways, one is conservative and accepting while the other is liberal and skeptical.[15] Lieutenant General S C Sardeshpande (Retd) is of the opinion that soldiers react 'intuitively' while media acts 'critically', which is true in both the cases. These characteristics are to be understood if one desires the synthesis and integration between the two. Only then the synergetic employment of both will be achieved.

Defence and security consciousness level in our country has risen and the Indian media turned out to be a force-multiplier during Kargil conflict. Kargil proves that there is still a need for greater interaction between the media and the military on a regular basis, and at deeper levels.[16] Ajai K Rai, a journalist and a researcher, feels that the media in future wars be allowed greater access to the areas of operations, and there must be greater confidence between the commanders and the media.[17] For this to happen, we must endeavour to understand each others' ethos, working environment and the peculiarities before we commit ourselves to an environment where the convergence of objectives contributes towards the betterment of the society and the nation as a whole. Keeping in view the same, an effort has been made in subsequent chapters to explain the ground realities of the military as relevant to the media and the environment that pertains to the media for the benefit of the armed forces. A case study of the battles at Kargil is carried out in the subsequent part of the book before finally arriving at some conclusions. As one of the most deplorable and tragic of all human weaknesses is undoubtedly our total incapacity to look into the future, which is in sharp contrast to so many of our gifts, our skills and our knowledge;[18] we must endeavour to look into the future by analysing our past.

References

1. General Shankar Roychowdhury (Retd), Former India's Chief of the Army Staff on a TV discussion in the initial stages of Kargil Conflict.

2. Leena Parmar, "Kargil War and the Mass Media", *Armed Forces and the International Diversities* (Jaipur : Pointer Publishers, 2002), p. 319.

3. Dr DeWitt C Ellinwood, "A Perspective on the Western Front by An Army Officer from India", *Stand To: The Journal of the Western Front Association*, January 2002, p. 31.
4. *Ibid.*
5. Traditional folklores of *Ala Udal* battle stories in the form of poetry is one of the examples.
6. Sqn Ldr RTS Chinna (Retd), Center for Armed Forces Historical Research, USI of India, New Delhi.
7. Arvind Kumar, *Encyclopaedia of Mass Media and Communications,* Vol. IV, p. 143.
8. n.7.
9. "Kargil Martyrs: Uniting India", *The Kashmir Times*, 26 July 2000.
10. Lt Gen S C Sardeshpande (Retd), "Military and Media", *USI Journal*, Vol. 122, No. 510, (October-December, 1992), p. 496.
11. "Deterring Information Warfare: A New Strategic Challenge", *US Army War College Journal*, 96-97 (Winter), *NDC Papers* 3/97, p. 103.
12. Brig Daljeet Singh, "Information Warfare at the Strategic Level", *NDC Papers* 3/97, p. 107.
13. Lt. Gen Bernard E. Trainer (Retd), "The Military and the Media : A Troubled Embrace", Hedrick Smith (Ed), *The Media and the Gulf War – The Press and Democracy in Wartime* (Washington, D.C.: Seven Locks Press, 1992), p. 70.
14. *Ibid*, p. 71.
15. *Ibid*, p. 72.
16. Ajai K Rai, *Kargil Conflict and the Role of Indian Media*, IDSA, Delhi Papers-17, p. 109.
17. *Ibid.*
18. Ivo Andric, *"The Bridge on the Drina"* (1945), downloaded from www.worldaffairsmonthly.com on 24 March 2003.

1

Media : A Force Multiplier

The phrase 'force multiplier' is used in the military terminology as equivalent to something that adds synergy; an overall contributor to the effort where the sum of the parts is more than the whole. A force multiplier, when present, enhances the total effect of the constituents. One of the examples is the use of Air Borne Warning and Control Systems (AWACS) during the war. With the use of AWACS, correct and timely information about the enemy activities is available to the forces on ground and in the air. Defensive and offensive operations could be launched more effectively. Similarly, with adequate knowledge of each other's vulnerabilities and strengths, media and the military can immensely benefit from each other. It does not necessarily imply that either of them will have to toe the other's line. The fear of the military is that the media in their exuberance and hurry to take the truth to the masses might jeopardise their future operations. On the other hand, the media does not wish to be seen working under the influence of the armed forces and wishes to be totally independent in its reporting. But both the aforesaid fears can be surmounted when greater knowledge of each other precedes all their actions that remain independent of the other party's influence.

During the two World Wars the British thought it fit to keep Indian public informed of the course of war wherein Indian soldiers' families benefited from the information flow. This in turn helped in keeping the morale of the soldiers at higher platform at the front.[1] Not only the native Indians were put at ease; the colonial British also derived mileage out of it in terms of better governance. Media continues to be a thermometer/ barometer/ mirror or the pulse of a society. The Press Council of India too had expressed similar sentiments when they called media a mirror of society and viewed it as a force-multiplier – not in the negative sense of being a propaganda tool but in the positive sense of boosting morale by presenting issues fairly and squarely with due responsibility.[2] Recognising the importance of media, General Shankar Roychowdhury, the former Chief of the Army Staff in his now famous 'Ten Commandments' to the Indian Army troops employed for low Intensity conflict operations had exhorted them to use media 'as a force-multiplier and not as a force-degrader'.[3]

Truth and Media

Senator Johnson way back in 1917 had remarked that, "*The first casualty when war comes is truth.*" often due to the vested interest, parties twist the truth to suit their needs. In the modern day techno-savvy media environment, it may paradoxically be difficult to hide the truth on one hand while on the other a convincing story can also be narrated hiding the truth, depending upon how free the media is. Media plays a very vital role in both the cases. In the first case, independent and unbiased media can expose untrue stories and thus make the propaganda machines of the parties involved ineffective. By doing so, the media ensures that the force multiplication effect of the propaganda is neutralised. While it may be the neutralisation of one side; for the other side it may very obviously result into a gain. What we are seeing is the negative and positive force multiplication taking place alongside when the media is not toeing line of any one of the parties involved in the conflict and ensuring that the truth is not getting distorted. In the second case, when the media plays in the hands of interested parties, propaganda might get you the victory even before the first shot is fired by merely demoralising the other side and breaking the will to fight. Propaganda or the so-called psy-war or information war might even create a situation amongst the local population that they might even rise against their own government and if not, at least support the cause of the other party. What would result is a tremendous force multiplication achieved through the media. Media, and especially the visual one, is very vital in any campaign. This is evident when one looks at the possible reasons of bombing the Iraq Television during the Gulf War in 1991 and the Serbian TV centre by NATO. Through denial and neutralising tactics on the media of your adversaries you prevent him any gain through his propaganda machine and, thus, achieve force multiplication.

Social Dimension

The attitude and commitment of people becomes vital to the conduct of military operations especially in the context of media glare.[4] It is, thus, very obvious that one must be concerned about the media to project a true and correct image to the public and once that is done, no matter what the odds are, a willing public support and response multiplies the chances of victory. It was in recognition of this fact that the late Chief of the Army Staff of the Indian Army, General B C Joshi, had called media a force multiplier.

Public support and national morale are powerful force-multipliers in themselves. General D Eisenhower shortly before the D Day landings in Normandy had said, "I believe that the old saying-'public opinion wins wars'-is true. Our countries fight best when our people are best informed."

To substantiate the argument, one needs to know what really are the elements that matter most during a war? Undoubtedly, superior strategy and sound ground tactics, bigger army with better equipment than its adversaries and inspiring leadership are but a few of the requirements to successfully fight a war. But to win a war a nation also needs the will of its people and the soldiers. If the people in general are not supportive of the cause of the war and adopt a couldn't-care-less-attitude towards it, the same attitude gets passed on to the soldiers, to the detriment of the force as such. History is replete with instances where the neglect of the popular will has cost many rulers their kingdoms and the best of generals, boasting of best of the armies, have lost the battles. What really emerges is *the importance of the elements of the will to fight and win* as one of the most important factors to win the war. If we go back to the available past scriptures in India, *Bhagwad Gita* offers to serve us a true example of what is just said. Seeing his kith and kin lined up against him in the battlefield, Arjun dithered, wavered and was unwilling to fight them. Lord Krishna, his charioteer, then stepped in to restore his will to fight. If you closely scrutinise the *Bhagwad Gita*, there are a total of eighteen chapters, out of which six chapters are devoted to *'will', 'emotion'* and *'cognition'*. Thus, the will of the people and, above all, the will and the state of the mind of the soldiers are extremely important if one does not wish to face defeat on the battlefront.

How does this will, emotion and cognition or the state of mind then relate to the topic being discussed? No one denies the role media plays in forming or evolving an opinion. That, in fact, is one of the fundamental roles of media besides providing information. Opinion creates a state of mind, which is precisely what constitutes the will and in other words is known as 'morale'. Many difficulties will be overcome with a high state of morale and if not, no matter how sophisticated the weapons are, victory on the battlefront will be elusive. Media plays a very vital role in peaking and sustaining the morale for duration of the conflict.

It is directly related to the adrenalin in the blood circulation. As a rule, morale cannot be at peak at all times. Bio-rhythms may not permit. However, a high plateau can be maintained. Morale has to be boosted. The soldiers need to peak just before the impending attacks, and sustain it during the Operations. Physiologically, they will return to their plateau on termination of the Operation. You need the media here for such a boost at the right time and to maintain the higher plateau at all times.

Media serves as a forward and backward link for the soldier. Most of the activities on the battlefield upfront generally reach the people back at home through letters, telephones and soldiers returning to their homes on leave. Perspective in its entirety however is unwholesome, as it would depend upon the person who narrates it. In some of the cases, such feedback may result into all kinds of rumours. When such rumours find their way back again to the front, the soldier's morale may be adversely affected. Mr BG Verghese very aptly puts it thus: "*Soldier is somebody's son, husband, father or brother and is connected to them, who in turn are connected to the society. The soldier is thus a part of the societal loop and anything effecting them, effects him too. Rumours spreading at home reach the front too and effect his morale. His emotional two days' leave can be very vital to the victory at the crucial moment.*"[5] Soldiers are not only connected to the people at home but are one of the corners of a triangle whose other end is connected to the government. People and the government in themselves are intricately intertwined, thus completing the triangle. Sensitivity of any one or more corners of the triangle would imbalance the whole system. Situation reports from the front are passed on backwards horizontally and vertically upwards in a hierarchical chain. At each stage an evaluation of the event takes place which not only consumes time but also may have certain additions or deletions depending upon the personalities involved. The result is that the output is somewhat different than the original chain of events. Also, it may have taken so much of time that to react upon the situation is either not desirable or just too late. Of course, there always are other channels through which urgent and important reports are forwarded, but such reporting is only applicable to the importance of the situation. Should we add media, another element, to this triangle, it would not be difficult to presume what may be the outcome. Media would act as a bridge between the military and the people, government and the military and last but not the least between the people and the government.

It would be pertinent to tabulate the kinds of media reports which reach the masses. Generally, the reports can be classified as :-

- Immediate. On the Radio and TV.
- Part analysed and part FIR. Daily newspapers.
- Analysed for general readers. Popular weeklies and journals.
- Militarily and strategically analysed. By IDSA,USI and such.
- Specifically researched. Books, research papers and post conflict papers.[6]

Let us now examine as to what will happen when the media starts reporting directly from the front. Stories from the battlefront will start reaching not only to the people in general but also the people in the government who are responsible for framing and implementing the policy. Firstly, an almost real time input about the latest happenings in the battle zone would be available and by the time the official version has reached them, there would at least be some homework done and time consumed would be reduced in the process. Secondly, the news from the front would not be totally raw, as some kind of analysis by the experts associated with the media would already have been done. Initial response of the people and a feedback would also be available. Thus, giving direction to the reactions and thereby not going wrong in responding to a situation, which might have far reaching consequences not only for the morale of the troops and people in general but also for the success of the operations on the battlefront.

Media – A Bridge

The role of the media to act as a bridge between the people and the government is well known and does not require an elaboration at this juncture. What is, however, important here is to state that in a war or a war like situation as that of Kargil, the efforts of the Government and the Armed Forces and the will of the people must all be synergised in a tandem to get the desired results. For easier reference in future, the role and reach of the media from the front is being termed as the 'backward sweep' and the sustenance of the morale of the soldiers on the battle front is termed as the 'forward sweep'. The sum-total of the two 'sweeps' is the synergetic gain.

While reiterating the points in favour of calling the media as a force multiplier, the motivation factor of the soldiers comes first as without it no victory is feasible. For correct policy formulations, it is important that fullest possible information is available to the makers of the policy. Media does supplement the same to a great extent. A constant cry of the public, expressed through the media, acting as a constant reminder and the access to the information makes for a good recipe for taking a timely decision. Another factor that is important is the weaknesses highlighted by the media that ultimately result in removal of the problems. A case in point is the lack of equipment and winter clothing for the soldiers involved in Kargil highlighted by the media. It made people aware to the facts of what soldiers wear on the frozen heights of the Himalayas. A positive outcome of the criticism followed and thereafter there were no obstacles in the clearance and sanction of such needs.

Defence Forces, Society and Government

The defence forces of any society or state, says Mr JN Dixit, have been endowed with self-confidence and discipline when they had a close relationship with their people and the civil government. Awareness of defence matters among the government and the citizenry, results in a positive relationship between the defence forces and civil society and makes the defence forces emotionally committed to the causes which they uphold . It also makes them strong in logical terms due to public awareness and public support.[7] Mr Dixit argues that what really matters is the relationship the armed forces enjoy with its civil societies and the awareness of matters military among the government and the civil society at large. He supports this argument by quoting some of the historically significant and extremely relevant military events. "*We must recall that Sparta emerged victorious against the other city states of ancient Greece during the Peloponnesian war in the 5th Century BC primarily because of the deep involvement of the people of Sparta with their defence forces. Athens and its allies were defeated despite greater resources and a larger army and navy because close relationship between the forces of Athens and its people did not exist. The ascendance of Rome as a strong state and an imperial power lasted as long as there was a close interaction between the defence establishment of the Roman Empire and the citizens of Rome. Historians attribute Rome's victory over Carthage to this particular factor. In the hind sight it could be even said that Rome created and sustained an empire stretching from England in the north to the Mediterranean and north western portions of Asia due to the positive equation between its citizenry and defence establishment. The decline of Rome commenced when this linkage between the peoples of Rome and its rulers and military leaders broke. The decline and ultimate fall of the Roman Empire can clearly be attributed to the self-centredness of Roman rulers and the Roman defence establishment in the last years of existence of the Roman Empire. The rulers insulating themselves against the peoples and the resulting Governmental policies having no correlation with the aspirations of the citizens resulted in the disappearance of one of the strongest powers of the ancient and earlier medieval powers of the world.*"[8]

The successes and failures of the defence forces are directly affected by the nature of their relationship with the civil society and the place they have in that society. Even more important is the enhanced awareness of civil society about their defence forces, and the mass media plays a very vital role in building it up.

Impact of Media on Military Operations

The impact of the media, especially the visual media, on military operations is becoming increasingly more important. Real time visual presentation can rapidly influence public and therefore political opinion.[9] Once the political opinion changes course, undoubtedly the military operations will need to be altered to conform to the latest thinking.

While analysing the impact of the media in all its forms and manifestations, one of the important issues in any operations that must not be ignored is the presence of a large number and a variety of stressors that the military commanders might face. Glynis Breakwell and Keith Spacie have summarised the key stressors and have divided these into four principal types:

- Organisational;
- Physical;
- Interpersonal;
- Psychological in a table on Taxonomy of Stressors.[10]

Media acts as one of the stressors and falls in the 'psychological' category. While amplifying the reaction to the media researchers have stated that: "*Commanders who are naturally reserved or concerned to control their public image may find interaction with the media a source of stress despite having been trained in interview skills, etc. They find it difficult because the whole process is antithetical to the way they like to exist in the social world. The pressure will be compounded if they are not sufficiently senior and can not curtail media access to them.*"[11]

Kargil was no exception. Due to media coverage stress did exist. Need to perform under constant-media-glare make matters stressful for any commander and it is more so during the operations. What is intended here is not to show that media affects as a force degrader. But, like presence of certain amount of positive fear is necessary for a brave act, similarly some amount of stress can act as a catalyst for greater performance of commanders on the battlefield and thus acting as a force multiplier. However, a caution is imposed in that it must be seen that the stress must not increase beyond the individual's capacity of tolerance and does not lead to his mental paralysis.

People in this part of the continent by nature are camera conscious. Presence of any one with a still or the video camera invariably makes them do things that they want to project about themselves. We see it happen often during weddings, when suddenly in front of the camera the behaviour of the person changes sometimes to the extent beyond our expectations. We also see it happen when the rioters on the street wait for the camera or the media to arrive to exhibit their anger or ire on a prevailing situation.

What makes them act in this uncharacteristic manner is the presence of the man holding the camera for the news coverage. Similarly, the presence of media on the battlefront encourages the soldier to act, but thankfully here, in a positive manner. Often the innocent questions like what is happening or what or where is the action scene today, when repeated a couple of times, brings the focus of the local commander to show some action, thereby adding to his stress level. It is not the stress level alone; a large or frequent congregation of media in one particular sector shifts the focus of operations to that area. If one particular place is in news with regularity, a debate is generated and in-turn it influences the mind of the decision maker. It, thus, not only affects the tactical conditions but also at times successfully alters the strategy of military operations, be it in a positive or negative direction. We have witnessed it taking place during the Kargil conflict; first the initial success in Dras sector drew the media to this area. Later, the constant presence of the media in Dras, as opposed to occasional visits of the media personnel to Batalik sector due to its comparative inaccessibility, completely shifted the pivot of action to this relatively small part of the battlefield. What we actually saw was the powerful impact or the influence of the media on conduct or the outcome of the operations. When the effect is positive and it contributes to the success, the media qualifies as a force multiplier and vice versa.

Media and Battlefield Control Spans

The control of the battle involves a complicated maze of actors and sub actors. Like a machine needs all parts well oiled and integrated with each other to achieve optimum performance, battlefield too needs the similar synergy in terms of integrated control. When all these actors and sub actors work in an environment free of friction, efforts put in multiply the output. If a catalyst is added it multiplies manifold the results achieved. A close scrutiny of the control spans in a battlefield will indicate the requirement of the presence of such a catalyst that has to be identified and harnessed to buttress the operational need. Media essentially qualifies to be a catalyst. We will now see as to how true this is.

There is a 'Horizontal Span of Control' as also a 'Vertical Span of Control' of the Operations in a battlefield. Horizontal Span of Control is defined by some analysts as the control of operations of one's command. For example, a Corps Commander is responsible for the control of operations of the three military divisions usually placed under his command; similarly, a Brigade Commander will control three or more battalions and employ them in the battlefield.

On the other hand, the Vertical Span of Control could be defined as those other binding parameters that are given to Horizontal Span of Control Commanders, that are meant to control the battle but are not at the discretion of these Commanders. The timings of the operations, availability of additional or special forces/troops and the depth up to which the operations could proceed, say crossing of the Line of Control are some instances.

Horizontal and Vertical Spans of Control bring us to various levels of commands in an organisation like the Army. At the lowest level there will be an executive class, who implement the executive orders passed through their senior commanders. At the narrow apex are the policy makers or the strategic planners, who jointly produce a workable plan of action. If one were to draw a hierarchy, all soldiers and all their commanders in the battlefield qualify to be part of the executive class. A narrow band of the senior commanders exist in the middle level who are instrumental in giving finesse to the strategy, co-ordinating and implementing the plan through the executive class. The apex will consist of organisations like the National Security Council or people like the Chiefs of the three Services, senior bureaucrats in concerned ministries and the various heads in the government.

Media, by its inherent organisation and work culture, will invariably be interacting with all the above mentioned levels almost simultaneously. At the same time, media will also be in a position to critically review any thing that may not be within the span of control of either of the two control spans discussed above. Such a position of the media often puts it in a position that could make the media qualify to be a catalyst. Media, if in tandem with the entire effort of the operations, could, thus, reap a rich harvest. All that is needed is little realignment and understanding of each other. Once that is achieved, force multiplication will automatically follow.

References

1. AK Sachdev, "Media Related Lessons from Kargil", *Strategic Analysis* (January 2000), p. 1799.
2. *Pen and Sword*, Press Council of India report, 1994.
3. *Ibid* and n. 1.
4. Brig Daljeet Singh "Information Warfare at the Strategic Level", *NDC Papers* 3/97, p.128.
5. BG Verghese in a meeting with the author on 1 March 2002.
6. Brig KS Gulia in discussion with the author.
7. JN Dixit, "Field Marshal Cariappa Memorial Lecture 1997", *Sainik Samachar,* 1-15 March 1998.
8. *Ibid.*
9. Wg Cdr TK Bhatara, "Media Management in the Services", *Defence Managemement* (November 1999–April 2000).
10. Glynis Breakwell and Keith Spacie, "Pressures Facing Commanders", *The Occasional Paper* (Number 29, 1997), Strategic and Combat Studies Institute, p. 26.
11. *Ibid.*

2
Ground Realities Within the Army Governing Interaction with the Media

Before an effort to analyse the relationship between the media and the army is made, the ground realities that prevail in a military environment must be understood. Key word linking the media with the military is 'information'. The main concern of the military is that the information, which could jeopardise a military operation or endanger the lives of the troops who have to carry it out, should not be published. The very first essential in any battle is to prevent any information of value falling in to the hands of the adversary, who in turn could utilise the same to his advantage. To ensure the secrecy of such a nature, the information that the Fourth Estate is bound to use needs to be vetted of its content and it does require a reasonable time, if not more, to do so. As opposed to the secrecy and its inherent requirements, media's main fields are wide-open publicity, speed and credibility of the information, thus leading to diverse considerations. For an effective force-multiplier that the media is, it is the job of military and media both to reconcile to these facts. Unquestionably, the information on the operations is the stuff of military secrets, but they are also the making for great stories of human endeavour, intrigue and struggle.[1] This organic difference between the military and media must be well understood by both the parties concerned and as the media tries to satisfy the needs of public, the Army must learn to satisfy the needs of media.

Organisational Difference

The military, institutionally, is mission oriented; and so is the media. Although, one may feel that their missions appear to be antithetical, it must be borne in mind that military as an organisation is an instrument of the government and is subject to all the external constraints that come along with it. Not only the external constraints, the situation often is compounded by all the internal restraints associated with a hierarchical structure. On the other hand media organisation is structurally slimmer, quicker and flatter with a preference for facts and views. Thus, at times, the situation arises where the conflicting requirements have to be accommodated in the overall interest of the nation to whom both are committed. More often than not, the situation can be altered for achieving far reaching dividends with minor adjustments; all that it requires is an understanding of each other and a will to accommodate each other's necessities.

Cultural Ethos

To know the army better, we have to first take into account that culturally the Army has inherent barriers to external communication as it remains in remote and far-flung places. The vocabulary and usage of words and phrases may mean something else in the civil street and may not be correctly interpreted by a common man. Living conditions are harsh and different than any other organisation. Obviously, such an environment generates different expectations, feelings and behaviour. Should we term these differences as good or bad is a matter of choice, as these simply exist and nothing much can be done to alter them. It may not be irrelevant to mention here that the national defence, military force, soldiering, armed forces, military organisations, strategy, tactics and weaponry are specialised subjects alongside humanities, science and technology. Military is an organismic being, not a robot of mechanical obedience.[2] Unless we have this basic knowledge about them and their psyche and ethos, we cannot be objective, accurate and credible in our reporting about them.

Image Consciousness

Like any one else, the Army too is image conscious. At a recent seminar on 'Media and National Security' held at IIMC, New Delhi one of the speakers remarked, "*Undoubtedly, the Armed Forces have a hallow around them as it should be. They enjoy tremendous admiration of the people. At the same time we must understand that the Armed Forces are extremely image conscious and sensitive to media criticism.*"[3] It matters to an individual as well as the organisation as to how their actions are perceived by others; as their strength lies in the support that they receive from the others in each and every action of theirs. It must be remembered that whatever actions a soldier takes in his professional capacity are for a just cause; for the security and integrity of his nation. He does not kill for earning additional remuneration or a promotion for himself as the integrity and loyalty to the nation always comes first and foremost, welfare of his men is the next. Before an officer takes the final step out from training academy, he is taught that his personal welfare and comforts come last. Morale of a soldier soars when he knows that he has the backing of the entire nation for a particular cause; he is even ready to lay down his life for the same. He does not waver while killing the enemy; and in doing so he knows that he may himself be killed. What takes him to such an extreme human behaviour; courage or self-indulgence? Obviously, it is the combine of his moral and physical courage that takes him ahead and this comes from the fact that he has the support of the people for whose sake he wore the uniform. Media plays an important role in garnering this support–in forming a bridge between him and the people.

Motivation and Morale

Motivation is another factor that has far reaching implications for a soldier at all times and it is the most important factor in the war. If he knows that the nation cares for him and his social needs and obligations such as his family are taken care of, he rises above his personal bondage. At no time he must be made to feel that he is a forgotten human specie, fighting in a Godforsaken piece of land for ungrateful people. The media takes him to the masses and assists him in sustaining his high morale and motivation. It requires responsible reporting by the media of the events of his daily life in peace stations[4] and more so on the battlefront. The upward journey from the proverbial 'morale in boots' to the 'morale touching the sky' needs sustained efforts which comes from training, sense of belonging, inculcating a sense of pride, cohesive team work and, above all, by exemplary leadership. Even a small event can bring down the spirits or can raise the morale if handled correctly. In a bid to report and to offer a critique, the implications of such a report or the critique upon the morale and the motivation of a soldier must always be kept in mind.

Rules and Regulations

Being an instrument of the government, the hierarchy in the military is subject to all the rules and regulations associated with it. The first and the foremost being the Indian Official Secrets Act, 1923 which has often been termed as an archaic imperial legacy.[5] There are representations from various quarters to amend the same. Quite a few armed forces officers too have expressed their views about the Act. One of them viewed Indian Official Secrets Act, 1923 as one of the legacies of the colonial era, and an obsession among the armed forces to avoid contact with the press. "*Whereas insularity was deliberately sought prior to 1947 through a desire to maintain the status of the armed forces as the holy cow*", he observed "*in a free and democratic society it invariably leads to misunderstanding and disinterest on the affairs of the armed services among the countrymen at large*".[6] That the Indian Official Secrets Act, 1923 is used as a tool by the armed forces to avoid the press is not entirely true. The fact that there is a rule laid down, is sufficient for the armed forces to comply with it. There is no question of disobeying it and any use of it cannot be termed as an obsession to use the same to avoid contact with the Press. Yes, the Indian Official Secrets Act could be reviewed for the sake of greater transparency by taking into account the current ground realities. Some even suggest that the Indian Official Secrets Act be scrapped. They feel that a new Right to Information Act, which should clearly demarcate the fields in which official secrecy would be permissible, should replace it.[7] In fact, it is said to have become an irritant to service officers themselves who have to redeem their pledge to conform to the provisions of the Official Secrets Act every two-years.[8] The point highlighted here is not to advocate the scrapping of the Indian Official Secrets Act but to amplify the imposition of restrictions on the armed forces and thereby modulation of interaction with the media. This fact has to be appreciated by all those who wish to interact with the armed forces.

Like every organisation has certain regulations governing the professional conduct of its members, the Army too has its code of conduct laid down in the Regulations for the Army. Communication to the press is not forbidden but it does have certain pre-conditions that must be fulfilled; basically to prevent breach of overall security. When objectively seen, it does imply imposing some caution on a soldier while he interacts with the media; which may not be liked by the other party. However, what may be said in support of the same is that it is somewhat similar to a journalistic norm of keeping the identity of his source hidden till it is essential.

Training About Media

Like the media is required to understand the basics of occupation, functioning, requirements and limitations of the armed forces, the military too must have knowledge about the Fourth Estate. This is one area where the military needs to stress upon. A young officer in his training period at the National Defence Academy, Khadakwasla; Indian Military Academy, Dehradun or the Officers' Training Academy at Chennai has hardly any exposure to the media. Of late, the Army War College, Mhow has introduced a new syllabus in which the officers attending the Senior Command Course are given a realistic exposure to interaction with the media in a fictive scenario. This is the first formal exposure to the officers about the media. The media, including the students of journalism from the neighbouring Indore City, have wholeheartedly supported this programme which is conducted once in every quarter in a year. The interaction becomes interesting that it generally overshoots the timings scheduled for it and invariably ends up with a sense of 'wanting more' by both the participants. Feedback received from the event suggests that such an interaction is extremely useful, both for the men in uniform and the journalists who participate in it. Army Training Command (ARTRAC), Simla has of late been conducting seminars that are being attended by army officers to educate them about the media and the related issues.

In the US Army, officers promoted to senior ranks are put through a special capsule, to train them to understand and interact with the media effectively. Some of our senior officers also attend the media orientation workshops at Indian Institute of Mass Communication (IIMC), New Delhi. But given the curbs on their interaction with the media in the earlier and formative years of service, often these workshops are a typical example of a case of too little and too late in life. It is to the credit of one of the senior officers[9], who confessed in a seminar held at the Defence Services Staff College some years ago that he had no exposure whatsoever in handling of media until he took over a Corps actively involved in counter insurgency operations. Others often echo similar sentiments. The essence of the whole idea is to lay the emphasis upon the 'lack of media exposure' for the men in uniform. Fortunately, now the efforts are on providing an institutional exposure about the media to the officers of the Indian Army. But more needs to be done, as the present effort may not be sufficient to meet the challenges of the interaction with the modern and technologically advanced media.

It is not only the lack of training about the media that makes the Armed Forces officers '*media-shy*', but also the emphasis during the training period to be accountable for what you do or say. What you say in public invariably has the tag of national security and its related matters. A minor twist to an innocent statement or innocuous remark may itself be catastrophic in terms of the career of the otherwise upcoming officer in question. Such a presumption on his part leads to his inability to freely interact and as such inaccessibility to the media. Although, one could argue that such a presumption is not an exclusive domain of the Armed Forces officer but is equally applicable to any person holding official responsibility. But, here lies the catch. What may be ignored elsewhere certainly is not pardonable here. The Indian society holds the Armed Forces in very high esteem and even a minor lapse makes for sensational news. Scores of examples can be quoted in support of this argument yet, are not deemed appropriate to be listed here. What can further be added is that for a guarded but meaningful response why not train them? The issues of training are elaborated in subsequent chapters.

Public Relations

Public Relations is one area where the military in India had taken a lead. Directorate of Public Relations (DPR) in South Block is one of the oldest public relations organisations in the country. DPR, under the Ministry of Defence (MoD), is working ever since the British days. High tide of their defence reporting has been during the Second World War, where the DPR personnel accompanied the troops and wore army uniform. The Centre for Armed Forces Historical Research (CAFHR), based at the United Service Institution of India, New Delhi, has a word of praise for the war/battle accounts as a result of the efforts made by the DPR.[10]

DPR is an umbrella organisation for maintaining interaction with the media and the public. The DPR is headed by the Director, an officer of the Indian Information Service and comes under the Joint Secretary (General) of the MoD on policy matters. The DPR is in a unique situation in that he is accountable to the Principal Information Officer (PIO). He is the Government of India's chief spokesperson, rather than to the MoD.[11] The Director is assisted by the three Services Public Relations Officers (PROs). PRO (Army) is in turn in touch with PROs at various levels and locations. Status wise, the PRO's ranking is too low in the Service hierarchy.[12] However, he forms a key link between the media, the Chief of the Army Staff and his Principal Staff Officers. A recent addition to the Army Headquarters is the Army Liaison Cell (ALC), which came in its present form during the Kargil battle.

Notwithstanding the above, there is an existing need to have 'media-savvy' PROs down to unit / sub unit levels.[13] It must be remembered that the future battlefield will be fashioned by low-intensity conflicts and limited wars, where higher Formation Headquarters will often be too far away to respond immediately to the demands of the media.[14] Of course, the job of the media is to report the news and they would continue to do so irrespective of the fact others prepare themselves to help them or not.

References

1. General Michael J Dugan (Retd), US Air Force, "Generals Versus Journalists", in Hedrick Smith (ed), *The Media and the Gulf War: The Press and Democracy in Wartime,* (USA: Seven Locks Press, 1992), p. 61.
2. Lt Gen SC Sardeshpande (Retd), "Military and Media", *USI Journal,* Vol. 122, No. 510 (October-December, 1992), p. 495.
3. Air Vice Mshl Kapil Kak (Retd), Minutes of Seminar *Media and National Security* held at IIMC, New Delhi, 27-28 September 2000, p. 51.
4. All stations where families of soldiers are permitted to stay along with them throughout the year can broadly be understood as peace stations.
5. *Pen and Sword,* Press Council of India report, 1994.
6. Maj Gen Deepinder Singh (Retd), while commenting on Indian Peace Keeping Force in Sri Lanka.
7. Ramesh Narayan Swami, IAS, "National Information Policy", *NDC Papers* 3/97, p. 25.
8. VC Natarajan and AK Chakraborty, *Defence Reporting in India, The Communication Gap* (NOIDA: Trishul Publishers, 2002), p. 175.
9. Col SK Sakhuja, "Media and Military-Some Lesser Appreciated Facts", *Combat Journal* (September 2001), quoting Lt Gen Ajai Singh (Retd).

10. Sqn Ldr RTS Chinna (Retd), CAFHR, USI, New Delhi, in conversation with the author.
11. Dinesh Kumar, *Soldiers and Scribblers- Media in Information Warfare: A Case Study of India,* Occasional Paper Series, IDSA, June 2001, p. 23.
12. VC Natarajan and AK Chakraborty, n. 8., p. 20.
13. "Role of Media", *Jammu and Kashmir Study Report,* USI, New Delhi, (March, 2003), p. 83.
14. *Ibid.*

3
Indian Media Environment

Indian media has characteristically come of age. With the advent of television-journalism, news and views have started to mobilise the opinion of the masses never witnessed before. Defence related issues, be it the Kargil conflict with Pakistan, Tehelka controversy, Agra Summit, war against terror in Afghanistan or cross-border terrorism, media has lapped it all up to dominate the headlines. Battle in Kargil offered a platform on which news coverage took a new and decisive turn. Kargil came as a defining moment for the media specially the television. News and views on defence matters displaced the passions for discussion on politics and social aberrations such as murder, rape and adultery. While the hold of films on entertainment retained its appeal, ardent love of Indians for cricket too suffered a crash, albeit for a different reason. A large number of defence experts have emerged into the foreground and debates on TV channels, newspapers, and magazines have become a staple diet for the common man. The Fourth Estate never had it so good where the number of Kargil stories vying for the top slot outnumbered the 'fillers'.

Under the full glare of the media, specially the television, Kargil crisis earned the nickname of India's first media war. For history is witness to people forgetting their differences and bonding for a cause due mainly to the electronic media – television.[1] What we witnessed was the grand arrival of television on the news scene. However, it did not displace the other media actors. Both, the television and the print, have their own utility. *"The day of the printed word"*, said Erwin Canham, *"is far from ended". "Swift as is the delivery of the radio bulletin, graphic as is television's eye-witness picture, the task of meaning and clarity remains urgent. People cannot and need not absorb meaning at the speed of light."*

Reach of Mass Media

Being a force-multiplier, mass media's reach and penetration has to be fully comprehended to know its true potential. There are almost 6.4 million television sets in cities alone in India.[2] Going by the latest viewership surveys, according to Dr N Bhaskara Rao, television reaches little over 50 per cent of population of adults against nearly 40 per cent of newspapers of all periodicity. This was hardly 15 per cent in early 1970s. He further adds that in rural India, interestingly, newspapers reach hardly a quarter of population against much less than 10 per cent 30 years ago. He summarises by saying that hardly one-sixth of adults are "heavy readers" – 25 per cent in urban and about 7 per cent in rural. Rao adds that English publications today have about 10 per cent readers against about 2 per cent 30 years ago. Readers of daily newspapers comprise 90 per cent of the total readers. Readership for magazines works out to hardly one out of every five and there has been a decline in the number of magazines.[3] However, if we combine all the methods of conveying information, today there is an information overload. News reaches all parts of the globe even before it is known locally. Therefore, to say the least, it would be fair to assume that the reach of mass media is phenomenal.

With a backdrop of mass media's extended reach and changes and shifts in media paradigm, understanding of media ethos, characteristics and the environment is essential for military, if a synergy between the two of them is to be achieved. Thus, it is prudent to ask the proverbial five 'Ws' and one 'H' about the media and discuss them very briefly before venturing ahead.

Constitutional Guarantee

Sir Winston Churchill had said, "*Free Press is the unsleeping guardian of every other right that free men prize.*" The first essential is that the constitution of a country must guarantee the Press the desired freedom. The Constitution of India has been drafted with utmost care and due thought given to all such essential needs. Let us begin with examining Article 19(1)(a) of the Constitution of India. It guarantees all citizens the right to freedom of speech and expression, which is basically one of the fundamental rights of a human being. Right to freedom of speech and expression to all the citizens also includes the media. In the Constitution there is no separate provision which deals exclusively with or guarantees the freedom of the Press. Freedom of expression as mentioned in the Constitution implies all forms of opinions, thoughts, ideas and convictions and, thus, covers most of what is needed for the freedom of the Press. In addition, general laws of the country are equally applicable to the Press in India and by evolution are also applicable to the entire media now. We, therefore, can safely conclude that the Constitution of India does cater for a free Press or free media.

Along with the freedom, certain restrictions too have been conceived for the Press. It must be noted that clause 2 of Article 19 enables the State to impose reasonable and justifiable restrictions on the exercise of the freedom in question. While comparing it with some of the other major democracies of the world what can be added here is that in the United States of America and Great Britain, the Press enjoys the freedom but without any special privileges. Primarily the freedom of Press in these countries implies no licensing or censorship of literature of any kind in times of peace. It may be interesting to know that Sweden probably is the most open society in the world where even the principles of free access to public document in addition to other freedoms was accepted through an act dating back to 1776.

A Code for Media in India

After having taken a cursory glance at the constitutional freedom of the Press, let us now make an attempt to know as to how the evolution of a code for the Press has taken place ever since Independence. The first Press Commission was set up in 1952 and it functioned till 1956. As a result of the recommendations of the first Press Commission, Press Council of India was set up in 1966. Also, an effort was made in 1953 to evolve a code for the Press. All India Newspapers Editors' Conference framed not only a 15 point code of ethics for all journalists but also an eight point Editors' Charter. It also laid down "Guidelines" for communal writings (Eapen 1989) in 1968. Later, the Emergency period in India saw a 14 point code.

The second Press Commission deliberated upon various issues in 1981 but did not frame a code straightaway. It argued that it could be built up case by case. The same year witnessed a 12 point Declaration of Journalists. Various other issues have thus been sought to construct the code of ethics, but, in essence, these are neither formalised nor do they have a legal status.

Press Council of India

The Press Council of India (PCI) is a statutory body with a self-regulatory mechanism. Its main job is to ensure the dignity of Press and observance of professional ethics by journalists. After the Emergency, the PCI was reconstituted in 1979. It comprises of 28 members – 20 from the Press, five from sitting MPs and remainder three from among eminent personalities. A retired Judge from the Supreme Court of India is appointed as its Chairman. This body wields a fair amount of moral power and legal authority. It adjudicates in respect of all complaints against or by the Press. It deals with journalistic ethics, values and standards and ensures that erring journalists are kept on the path of professional rectitude by their own peers. Thus, the Press in India seem to be well organised, powerful, responsible and governed by statutory and voluntary regulations to prevent its malfunctioning. However, in the past the PCI has often been criticised for its lack of adequacy. Some professionals in this field call it "a Paper-Tiger with rubber teeth"[4] or a "toothless tiger because of its lack of penal powers."[5] In India, several newspapers have not appointed an Ombudsman despite pressures from the Press Council.[6]

When we look at other constituents of the media, what emerges is that the print media has at least the intent but the broadcasting media, especially the television that geared up in the nineties had nothing planned for quite some time. One may infer that since All India Radio and Doordarshan, both Government of India undertaking, had been the sole broadcasters to the nation, a need to have a regulatory code had not arisen for obvious reasons. There were no private or commercial operators in this field until the 1990s. Progress to evolve a code or regulation has been slow and even now in the name of a code only Cable Network Regulating Programme exists. Meanwhile, Information and Broadcasting Foundation Task Force is drafting the ground rules for a regulatory mechanism, which shall soon be in force.[7] Ironically no licenses are required to practice journalism in our country like most other professions and there is seemingly a bit of void for want of rules.

Press Freedom Versus News Freedom

The slogan 'Press Freedom' has a contender in 'News Freedom'. We must examine as to what does it mean. After the period of investigative journalism initiated by late Dhiren Bhagat in reporting Indian Peace Keeping Force Operations in Sri Lanka and sustained by Bofors scandal by N Ram of the *Hindu* in Madras and Chitra Subramanian in Geneva, newspaper readers were beginning to be seen as nothing more than a market, and the information disseminated to them was simply a commodity or goods to be sold. Saleability of the paper through increase in circulation was what mattered.[8] The same trend has begun to emerge in the television today where capture-of-maximum-eyeballs matter the most. Commercialisation and sensationalism of the news with regular interference by private interests seem to be order of the day. One must not forget what Nehru had once said: *"Freedom of the Press usually means non-interference by the government, but there is such a thing as interference by private interests. The fact is that a big industry owning a newspaper or chain of newspapers can not be said to give the Press the kind of the freedom public expects from it."* India must guard against the "Press Freedom" which is presently beginning to assume the form of free "license" to print at will and instead, should give shape to the concept of "News Freedom" and "Information Accuracy".[9] Why is it that a free Press must still be wanting in news freedom? Answer probably lies in various push and pulls that are responsible for it.

Statistics giving details of all the pressures that work upon a journalist/editor are summed up in a Journalism Alumni Survey [Delhi 1988 (Eapen and Thakur, 1989)]. The survey covered all those who received professional education in journalism or communication in any Indian University and were employed by mass media. Of the 72 respondents 88.9 per cent "were not absolutely free to write and report as per their conscience". The percentage of pressures and interferences from various quarters are self indicative:-

- Proprietor–85.9 per cent.
- Government–82.2 per cent.
- Editors–70.3 per cent.
- Political parties–60.9 per cent.

- Advertisers–48.4 per cent.
- Trade Unions–26.6 per cent.
- Editors/journalists succumbed to pressures/yield to temptations–90.3 per cent.[10]

There is yet another ethical dilemma journalists often face that involves contesting claims between the peoples' right to know and on the other hand an individual's right to privacy. While some societies have tried to resolve such dilemmas through enactment of legal rules, others have relied on voluntary self-regulation since statutory principles, powers and penalties might involve too heavy a cost in terms of freedom of expression. While the self-regulation offers the media greater leeway for irresponsible behaviour, it can only work if certain pre-conditions are met. These among others include the willingness on the part of the media to heed to criticism and obey the unenforceable.[11]

Another view of media was evident in a recent Seminar on "Media Reporting on Security and National Interest and Need for Self Regulating Mechanism", at India International Center, New Delhi. A renowned editor of a weekly magazine[12] considered the media to be truly responsible to the public and not to the Government and thus absolving themselves from the pressures from these quarters. He added that an editor must always look forward to the legitimate interest of the public in accepting a sound story. However, as John Merrill in his article "Media Ethics in Asia" observes: there is but one overriding trans-national ethical norm that journalists everywhere should be truthful, unbiased and thorough in their reports; this must remain at the back of a journalist's mind.[13] By doing so he would automatically ensure freedom of news.

Role of Media

Traditionally, the newspaper's basic roles have been to inform, influence, entertain and foster the development of economy through advertising. Another role is to serve people and help make their lives better.[14] In other words, the media's role is that of news evaluation, analysis and assessment, and dissemination.[15] It must also be understood that a newspaper is a business institution and thus has a dual role. It is a quasi-public institution and a free enterprise.[16] The same can also be said about the electronic media. However, the problem begins when the mass media overlooks its responsibility to the public at large and emphasises more on being a free enterprise. A journalist, whether from a newspaper or a TV channel, performs two functions: reporting the news and offering interpretation and opinion based on news. A journalist might also write an account that is both entertaining and newsworthy.[17] Here comes the catch; what is news worthy and what is not? Who decides what is the news and what should be the headlines? Also, it must be seen as to what news need not be published or broadcasted. The role of a journalist is not that of a detective as such or a historian but to use his eloquence to convey to his readers all about the event. He is merely an imaginative onlooker and not a participant.[18] Major General Winant Sidle of the US Army says, *"The appropriate media role in relation to the government has been summarised aptly as being neither a lap dog nor an attack dog but, rather, a watch dog."*[19]

In the Jammu and Kashmir Study Report (USI), the role of media has been stated to be:-

- To create public opinion.
- Act as watch-dog for citizens, especially on human rights issues.
- Keep the public informed, with balanced coverage of events; and
- Maintain national morale by giving responsible news reports.[20]

Let us also see as to what constitutes the 'news'? Paul White has called the news as an accurate and timely report of some event, situation, conditions or opinion; a report which will interest the particular persons for whom it is intended. Arvind Kumar defines it as the statement of freshly ascertained facts about something that has happened, is happening, is about to happen or that, contrary to expectations has not happened, and probably will not happen. Major General Patrick H. Brady wrote in *Army* magazine; *"Some look on news as just another four-letter word, but I believe it is more useful to look at it as a C-letter word: chaos, confusion, conflict, contradiction, crime, corruption, color, catastrophe. It does not hurt if you add some Ss – sex, sensationalism, state secret – to it. Information must be timely if it is to be news. Being first with Cs and Ss is the stuff of which news is made."*[21]

While working on the gathering of news, it is fair to presume that the journalist on ground is doing his homework assiduously and is investigating the subject holistically. It is also expected that he will make an accurate and unprejudiced report to his editor. It is now the editor's turn, who will decide to put it in its appropriate place. He is going to see the importance of the news, the interest it is going to create, its timeliness and unusualness. Emphasis may also be laid on stories that affect large numbers of persons and that involve their local communities. Their traditions, sources and advertisers also affect media's selection process.[22] It must be seen that stories going against the national interest must never be published however big a scoop it may be. Two competing public interests – the people's right to know and their trustees' duty to preserve secrets whose disclosure would harm public interest–must be balanced.[23] When you come to the very strong dilemma between the truth and national interests, the examples of British in Falklands and the Americans during the Gulf War may be kept in mind.[24] Civilian societies in both the countries have willingly accepted on not insisting on the truth but subscribing to national interests. People of the two societies have sacrificed their demand for the right to know in the interest of the nation.[25] It may naturally happen here in India or as a result of the manipulations by the people in authority, as some Indian TV journalist put it succinctly. At the same time, it must be remembered (and as the Press Council of India terms it) that the media has an 'adversarial role' to the extent that it questions authority, all authority, to look at the other side. This must be understood and a relationship of creative tension accepted as a democratic necessity. For the rest, they are partners in trying to build a better society.

Media Doctrine

The right of the public to know, rigid adherence to the facts and fairness in reporting are termed as the doctrine of the media by Manoj Joshi of *India Today* Group. Some of the standards of mass media as have been listed in *Encyclopaedia of Mass Media and Communications* by Arvind Kumar are reproduced below:-

(a) Profitability.

(b) Audience satisfaction.

(c) Accuracy.

(d) Objectivity.

(e) Unusualness.

(f) Relevance.

(g) Completeness.

(h) Independence.

(j) Propriety.

(k) Comprehensibility.

(l) Uniqueness.

Credibility and objectivity flow from the above as some of the prime standards and timeliness is what a defence journalist is most worried about when he is covering an event related to the Armed Forces. It is more often then not here that the problem arises. Getting the story often is not a problem in a war zone but to make it credible and despatch it before the deadline crosses is a recurring problematic phenomenon for a defence correspondent or a journalist; because to get past the hierarchy requires unusual tact.

Defence Journalism

To understand the environment a little better, let us get to what 'defence-journalism' implies. Defence journalism requires reporting on the military aspects of any country, keeping in mind the media's commitment to bring light aberrations, injustices, and irregularities, along with their achievements and contributions to society.[26] Defence journalism is one area where an inadequacy has been felt. Dinesh Kumar has this to say about the language Press: "*With respect to media-military relations in India, a major infirmity within the media is that most Indian language newspapers do not have dedicated defence reporters. This is unfortunate because it is these newspapers which are truly the common man's newspaper and play an important role in formulating public opinion. Also, defence reporting tends to be Delhi-centric. There are hardly any defence correspondents or reporters who understand issues and are posted in insurgency-affected areas where the army is involved.*"[27]

However, some television channels, newspapers and magazines now have dedicated experts on defence matters who contribute to this field in a near regular frequency.

Like a film artist whose market value is as good as his last film, a journalist is as good as the day's story and is on trial every day. Some senior journalists even refer to most journalists in India as generalists.[28] According to them not many are specialists, as the concept of specialisation is relatively new, though it is gradually picking up. Media is really not as institutionalised in the same way as the three pillars of any vibrant democracy are. It may be worth noting that the journalists are not recruited through institutionalised procedures like in the case of the Armed Forces or for that matter, even the executive, the judiciary and the legislature. It is not unusual, therefore, that often the media is accused of being all-powerful and having little accountability.[29] A greenhorn journalist, thus, when employed to report on defence matters, does have a disadvantage. His or her lack of experience to understand the linkages between the military tactics and the strategic environment results in a gap. Although, senior editors with an experience to back up their professionalism do ensure nothing inappropriate skips through their notice. A word of caution is, however, in order as even a minor lapse may cost many soldiers their lives.

To bridge this gap, the Directorate of Public Relations (DPR) (Defence) had initiated a programme in which a course was to be run at the College of Combat (now renamed as Army War College), Mhow for six weeks for the defence journalists who were below the age of 35. Basically, it afforded a journalist the opportunity to know the Army better by way of a brief on the structure, functions, weapons and the state of preparedness. Also he had the opportunity to interact with a large number of serving junior and senior level officers from all the arms and services of the Army, who came from all over the country. Vacancies on the course still exist but with only a few or no takers around. There was a proposal to include TV journalists and photographers as well on this course, but despite an open offer to the media, the course had to be stopped in 1992 till 1995 when once again it resumed with all its vigour. Unfortunately, only about 35 or so have undergone this 'war correspondents' course' so far over the last decade. As per media, the course has fallen short of their expectations on certain grounds. Some of them have even mentioned it in their writings that the course falls far short of the requirements of media in acquiring more knowledge about the operational element of all the three Services.[30] They have further stressed the need for the correspondents undergoing this course to be taken to operational areas arguing that it is not necessary that everything known to the press should be on the record or published. Most of the information could be useful subsequently when the need arises to report on action by the defence or security forces in sensitive areas of the country. No doubt it was a valid suggestion but what about the contribution in terms of sparing the correspondents themselves, which remained unpredictable till the middle of the course and when some of them joined the courses when they were finishing.

One can well agree with Dinesh Kumar when he says that to understand the profession of journalism it must be borne in mind that just as sealing the border is a myth, so is objectivity in journalism. According to him - journalists are expected to balance a news story with facts and, wherever applicable, round it off with comments from as many angles as possible. They are expected to view an event or an issue dispassionately. But this is not always done, and owing to various limiting factors, may not always be possible either. 'No news' is often described as 'good news'. But, journalists are often accused of reversing the cliché and treating good news as no news. News, as earlier described, is about the unusual, and to an investigative journalist, news is often seen as 'something that some one wants to hide. The rest is an advertisement'. Such an approach also makes newspapers and journalists susceptible to sensationalism.[31] Military operations are at times effected by the sensationalism; it creates an undue pressure upon the military commanders, who get worried to apply their combat strength to an area which they could possibly temporarily ignore for a gain in another tactical or strategic option. Such pressures must not be allowed to continue in a battle where heightened political sensitivity to public opinion and media reporting can encourage pressure on the military to generate short term tactical success for home consumption irrespective of the irrelevance of the action to the main effort. At the same time, it must be remembered that comparatively innocent news, when given a sensational turn, may lose its originality and the truth may be distorted causing irreparable damage. One of the veteran journalists has summarised the sensationalism in media thus:- "*To sum up: Both the print media, that is our daily newspaper and the electronic media, the TV channels, play up the sensational rather than the truth which is difficult to project. Whether, it is easier or more-audience attracting and therefore more advantageous than going over narrow and straight path, the media prefer the easy way out as it is reckoned beneficial because it attracts more readers and viewers and therefore more revenue."*[32]

Notwithstanding the above, what is seen is that on their part media does exercise caution and discipline while giving currency to the news related to the defence forces; however, at some stage it tends to peter out.

Media Coverage of Military

Media is an art of communication where the journalists use their eloquence to convey an event or a happening. Truly speaking, it is a constructed form of communication. Conversely, it must also be remembered that what can be constructed, can also be deconstructed.[33] Media coverage of the military can really be divided into four phases,

- Peace time period.
- Pre conflict period.
- Actual conflict period.
- Post conflict period.[34]

India has fought five wars; one with China in 1962 and four with Pakistan in 1948, 1965 and 1971 and now the latest is the limited conflict in Kargil during the summer of 1999. Indian military has also seen action on foreign soil during the late eighties by dispatching more than four Divisions of the Indian Army as the Indian Peace Keeping Force (IPKF) in Sri Lanka. The Indian Army, more than any other army in the world, has truly got a varied and first hand experience in handling counter-insurgency operations. Since the early fifties, the Army first dealt with insurgency in the North Eastern states, later in Punjab from mid 1980s to early 1990s and is now engaged in Kashmir since 1989. In addition, on a number of occasions in the past, the Army has also been called out in aid to civil authorities on internal security matters. Besides, the Indian Army has also been contributing troops for the United Nations in undertaking peace-keeping operations in various parts of the globe ever since independence and has earned a good name for itself.

All these engagements make for news and what is written about them or conveyed through the media effects not only the soldiers but also the common men in the streets. Whether it is pre, post or during the conflict or even during the peace period, the reporter or journalist requires a true understanding of the organisational and functional aspects of the defence forces to be able to do justice to his/her story. A great deal has been written in the media about the defence forces and their role during the past. To understand the role media played in reconstructing these battles, and before an analysis of the latest operations in Kargil is done, it may be prudent to briefly see as to how the media depicted some of these engagements.

Defence journalism in India can be traced back, according to VC Natarajan and AK Chakraborty, to 1909 when *Fauji Akhbar,* a journal of the British Indian Army, was founded.[35] The role played by the Directorate of Public Relations in the Second World War to bring out an authentic account of Indian soldiers on various fronts must be noted. War accounts like *Tiger Strikes* are true masterpieces of defence reporting.[36] Newspapers and the All India Radio had been the mainstay in the news reporting till the arrival of Television in its present form in mid 1990s. Till the 1971 operations, it was largely a government-controlled broadcast media. Presence of the foreign media in the war zone in Bangla Desh (then East Pakistan) presented a need to have a body that could represent the Indian viewpoint and, thus, the Press Information Bureau was conceived. With satellite television reaching the masses through the cable networks and the mushrooming of news channels, a fresh requirement to review the media policy is well on the cards. To analyse the defence reporting prior to this period, thus, only takes us to the evolution and the historical perspective of it. Lessons, although cannot be ignored yet the future perspective points to greater examination and analysis of the recent conflict in Kargil.

Sino-Indian War 1962

In 1962, the general public was vaguely aware of the emerging tensions between China and India on the issues of the boundary and the status of Tibet. The common man's perception suffered from the "Hindi-Chini Bhai-Bhai" syndrome and there was a lack of public awareness about Chinese incursions and Chinese threat. It was only after the conflict occurred and after our defeat that the Parliament and the people of India were able to take full cognisance of the happenings between 1959 and 1962.[37] Journalists were kept far away from the scene of action and what they got was inadequate information that lacked the details they would have liked to include. The media could not provide to the public an accurate picture of the situation in NEFA during the war. Media persons had to be content with sitting in Tezpur and receiving official handouts. As a result, rumours and facts intermingled freely in the media coverage of the war.[38]

Indo-Pak War 1965

Perhaps the right lessons were learnt from the experiences of the 1962 War and, therefore, in 1965 and 1971, the situation was quite different. The media was provided access to the forward areas and every effort was made to keep up the smooth flow of information.[39] Like in the previous war, the Radio and the Press were the only two sources of information to a common man. In the Press and over the Radio, there flowed a continuous stream of inspiring news items extolling the deeds of the men in the frontline.[40] The Press was briefed at South Block by the DPR and the journalists traveled only up to the rear areas of the battlefield until the cease-fire was declared. Hallmark of the role played by Indian as well as Pakistani media was the "hate campaign". In 1966, when the Tashkent Declaration was signed by India and Pakistan, after a three week war between the two, one of the points that preoccupied the negotiators was that both the countries put an end to the "tension building" or provocative role that the mass media of respective countries was playing in Indo-Pak relations.[41]

Indo-Pak War 1971

Public awareness between East Pakistan and West Pakistan and the likely role that India may have to play in managing this critical development steadily increased from December 1970 right upto 3 December 1971 when the war broke out with Pakistan and when we directly intervened in what was then East Pakistan. Not only was there deep and up to date awareness of the issues involved and the options that India could exercise; there was willingness to support the government and the defence establishment for the political and military initiatives which India took to meet the crisis. Informed and enlightened cooperation between the politicians, the civil services and the Armed Forces, backed by public support, constituted a unique example of a successful security and strategic exercise by India.[42]

Indeed, 1971 War was a classic and successful media and military interface albeit not without many problems.[43]

Indian Peace Keeping Force in Sri Lanka

In 1987, the Indian Army went into Sri Lanka to enforce a peace agreement signed between the Sri Lankan and Indian governments. Four Divisions of the Army, officially designated as the Indian Peace Keeping Force (IPKF), remained in the island country for nearly three years fighting the Liberation Tigers of Tamil Elam (LTTE). This engagement, called *Operation Pawan,* is often termed as India's Vietnam.[44] As per AK Sachdev, 1987 (also) saw the beginning of constricted defence information flow. He adds in the same breath that in the recent years, that trend has been somewhat reversed with the military becoming 'media savvy' and acknowledging the importance of good Public Relations (PR).[45]

The Indian as well as the Sri Lankan media regularly covered the IPKF operations. As compared to the Indian media, the media in the Island nation devoted larger time and space in their dailies, radio and the television. *Roopvahini,* the Sri Lankan television showed pictures of IPKF, Sri Lankan Army (SLA) and the LTTE quite regularly.[46] Indian media, on the other hand, limited themselves to reporting from a distance. There were no defence or war correspondents present on ground dedicated to get a first hand account barring a few exclusive reporters who came and went back. The matters were further compounded by the 'adversarial' reporting by Indian correspondents on IPKF operations in that island country.[47] To add insult to injury, towards the end of the operations, the Sri Lankan media started its own campaign of no love lost for a force which they often compared with an 'occupation army'. IPKF returned to the mainland not before it suffered large number of casualties. It was a case of media and military interface what ought not to be, specially now that one can compare it with the media coverage of the American war on terrorism in Afghanistan or in Iraq.

Media Management

According to one expert on the military intelligence, "media management has been the buzzword in the Army in recent years."[48] Jean Dreze is of the opinion that interest in media management tends to be at its peak in periods of active conflict, such as Kargil crisis, when winning the "information war" and using the media as a 'force multiplier' were explicit strategic objectives.[49]

On the other hand, media really abhors the idea of management of news by calling it the very anti-thesis of the freedom of Press. Natarajan and Chakraborty spelt out the doctrine of news management given as the norms and guidelines to them at the War Correspondent Courses in their book *Defence Reporting in India: The Communication Gap*. These guidelines suggested to them what could or could not be mentioned in a Press copy and what were the forbidden subjects in their photo coverage. It seems these guidelines were misunderstood; as is evident when one calls them 'self defeating and contradictory norms possibly dating back to the British days in Second World War'. It must be emphatically added here that what was tactically true of the armies in the Second World War days is true even today. For example, the side which had the correct information of its adversary was better prepared to win the battle. Operational plans (past, present or future) if known to the enemy would certainly jeopardise the success of an impending operation as was evident in Kargil. Imagine what would have happened if the Press in Pakistan had published all the details of the incursions by the Pakistan Army before they were even detected? Therefore, as Jonathon Alter has said, there's *a big difference between the right to do something-and the right thing to do.*[50] We must not misconstrue the true spirit of these guidelines as these are not meant to reign in media but to safeguard the interest of the Army in particular and the nation in general. The fact that all five American television network Channels (ABC, CBS, CNN, Fox and NBC) had agreed to comply with the US National Security Advisor Condoleezza Rice's directive to show restraint while carrying news from the Al Qaida network of Osama bin Laden, further substantiate the point at issue.[51] US media offered a sanitised coverage. As Siddharth Varadarajan wrote, *"Flickering lights on a distant horizon is how most people here are getting to see the US war against Afghanistan... as in the Gulf war, the Pentagan's media management is efficient and seamless without giving the impression of being obtrusive."*[52]

If we now look at the western media coverage of the recent war in Iraq, the point about imposing restrictions on media or management of media gets further reinforced. However, there is bound to be criticism if it crosses a certain threshold. According to the experiences of Delhi based Syrian journalist, Dr Waiel SH Anwad, who in order to cover the latest Iraq war had embedded himself with the US Troops, he was used as a decoy by the coalition forces. They were also made to sign documents restricting what they could report, and also absolving the US Army and government of any liability in case of death and injury.[53] VS Gupta wrote in *Vidura* magazine: *"Whereas the CNN, and to an extent even BBC became a part of the vast US establishment, it was the Qatar based television channel Al Jazeera, whose role in covering the war in Iraq dispassionately, was greatly applauded."*[54]

It must always be borne in mind that media not only does not like to be managed but also does not like it to be seen as being managed.[55] In other words, the media does not like itself to be 'used' by the people in authority as it was supposedly used in the case of Jessica Lynch in Iraq war. Stage management of an event or creating one for the sake of media to cover it in a manner that it serves some other purpose, could well be avoided as it neither is acceptable to the media nor does it auger well for their credibility and objectivity. VS Gupta, while offering his comments on covering the war in Iraq, says, "That objectivity and impartiality in reporting has been a casualty comes out in full force through the portrayal of a defining moment in war – statue of Saddam Hussain being toppled from its plinth in the Central Baghdad Fardous Square. That event has been telecast over and over again as the vindication of the stand of those who had planned the invasion of Iraq."[56]

Relationship : Media and Military

All over the world now, military institutions have embarked on a new relationship with the media, since the media moulds national and international opinion, and is a potent multiplier. In this century, they will need each other more than before. This does not apply to electronic media alone but also to the print and vernacular media. In fact it is said that in the 21st Century, an eye for public relations and military intelligence will be a major component in the selection of higher military assignments.[57]

Before proceeding to discuss the Indian environment, it would be worthwhile to know as to what General Andrew J Goodpastor (USA), former Supreme Allied Commander, Europe, had to say about the relationship between the media (western) and military, "*While there is-or should be-a natural convergence of interests in providing to the public accurate information about our armed forces and what they do, there is at the same time an inherent clash of interests (especially acute when men are fighting and dying) between military leaders responsible for success in battle and for the lives of their commands, and a media intensely competitive in providing the readers and viewers with quick and vivid 'news' and opinion.*"[58]

As perceived in the West, friction between the military and the media will continue to some degree in the future in the West. Professor Loren Thompson of Georgetown University aptly puts it: "*Even if the dilemmas of war coverage are fully appreciated on both sides and journalists and soldiers develop a sympathetic view of each other's need and responsibilities, friction will persist. Tension between major public institutions is inherent in the functioning of democracy, and it is not surprising that such tension is most pronounced in a setting where lives are lost and national interests are at stake.*"[59]

Unlike in the western world, the relationship between the media and the military in India is certainly not what it is thought out to be. Herein lies the difference. Certain thumb rules which may be true elsewhere do not universally apply to the media in India; which has an Indian character and identity. Media, of course, no more treats the Indian Army as a holy cow as was the case till some time back.[60] Not long back a newspaper wrote, "*Cariappa once described the Indian jawan as the 'salt of the earth', it is tragic that we now have to ask if his officers are worthy of him?*"[61]

However, not withstanding the aberrations, the media respects the military and acknowledges the compulsions and the hardships, unique in their own senses, it faces in India. Media emphasises the national pride in a professional non-political defence force which is truly national in its composition, role and outlook and considers the defence forces above the day-to-day controversy that surrounds so much else of national life. A quote from *The Statesman*, 15 March 2002 would further amplify the military value system that is honoured by the media: "*Serving the Indian Army – in the larger sense of term – has been hailed as a matter of honour simply because its sinews and strengths were forged by a set of values. Officers commanded not by the powers vested in them by the manuals but by sheer personal qualities. Their men had complete faith and trust in them, they would follow them into the jaws of death. It was moral authority at its most noble."*

Notwithstanding the positive inclination of the media towards the military, there are certain areas in which the media in India, in particular, finds the interaction with the military difficult. Certain impediments to military-media relations are existing. First, the government/military establishment has yet to fully appreciate the power of information and the role of media in policy making. And next, the media does not respect the social borders and taboos of the past. It is inspired by its own goals, and will go to any lengths to get news to the people – the consumers of information – who deeply resent any government control over the media. Holding back information and banning the media from sensitive areas alone leads to bizarre reporting, because media must report something![62]

There also are two major indefensible curbs on the people's right to know about their defence policies and preparedness that are not in tune with the media's thinking. One of them is the cult of secrecy practised by the successive governments since independence and the other; the Official Secrets Acts, 1923. Both are a hangover of the colonial era.[63] As a result, excessive preoccupation of the military; an instrument of the Government, with secrecy results in over-classification of information, which not only keeps the domestic public ill-informed on security matters but may also lead to the danger of dis-information and news manipulation. Because of the security restrictions, media men have to resort to obtaining news from unauthorised or ill-informed sources to be in time to push the story. Frequently, such reporting turns inaccurate. Often, such inaccuracies have to be corrected or denied by the agency reported upon, thus, creating a chain of avoidable events. Journalists have often pointed out the insensitivity of the military to the need to share information on a basis of trust. Even when newsmen gather information, *Defence of India Rules* and other laws are invoked to prevent publication of news and articles even though no security breaches are involved.[64] Most of the journalists feel that undue stress on the secrecy is redundant as in today's environment most of the information is available either in various publications the world over or on the Internet. Satellite imagery now even makes the military deployment available to any one who wants it and is willing to pay for it. BG Verghese observes: "*While the people remained in the dark, the whole world gets to know about the state of national defence through its intelligence network, satellite, military sales and transfer of technologies.*"[65] AG Noorani too had expressed views earlier in a similar context when he said, "*The Institute of Strategic Studies Islamabad (Pakistan), published in 1987 a study entitled Indian Armed Forces which provides a fund of authentic, sourced information on Indian Armed Forces. The authors Tariq A Hussain and Major Rafique, provide not only a chapter on each of the three services but also one each on higher defence organisation, defence production and on the nuclear and space programmes. All this in one slim volume of 128 pages for a mere Rs.30 (in Pakistan's currency). One can not help asking why the Annual Reports of the Ministry of Defence of India cannot provide such information to the people of India about Indian Armed Forces.*"[66]

Not much has changed. International magazines on defence give a regular update on the Indian defence expenditures, acquisitions and production. Therefore, is there a case to keep so many things still a secret in India? As a matter of fact one of the views is that India must rather create a mood of sober confidence without fear or panic in the people of the country. To discourage adventurism and miscalculations, says Verghese, it is important that an adversary should have a credible appraisal of India's strengths and preparedness. Any secret has a shelf life and in any case, he added, the best way to keep a secret is to tell it to the press.[67]

Another important media view about military is that the latter considers only the 'Olive Greens' to be patriots. Media is equally patriotic and even nationalistic while reporting in times of crisis. Once trust is placed upon media men, his or her professional ethics does not allow him to belie it. The interest of the nation would remain paramount in all his reportage.[68] During the 1971 Operations, some one in the media opined that; "*Treat the media with respect and confidence, let them feel they are an essential part of the larger scenario, tell them what the truth is and what is confidential, they will not betray a confidence or not go along with your failings and inadequacies and not appreciate your difficulties or not be grateful for your facilities.*"[69] Late General K Sundarji commented on similar lines: "*In an active war situation some information has to be kept under wraps for a duration, till certain plans unfold. Here again my own experience has been that the media, whether the print or electronic, by and large, plays ball when taken into confidence."*[70]

There are different views about the nationalism or patriotism displayed by the media; suggesting no sacrifice of objectivity and a neutral stand taken. However, such an attempt by a journalist may be misconstrued as anti-national. Rajdeep Sardesai, the Political Editor of New Delhi Television (NDTV) had once remarked; *"During Kargil anyone who questioned the government's intelligence failure was immediately labelled anti-national... in this age of insecure nationalism we are expected to show only what is in the 'national interest'. Any one who doesn't mouth old platitudes is branded anti-national."*[71]

A constructive and healthy criticism of a government policy must be positively regarded and accepted. Mr George Fernandes, Defence Minister of India acclaimed D R Mankikar's tall media stature and his book *The Guilty Men of 1962* at the India International Centre, New Delhi on 8 August 1998. He used a quote from this book, which would further substantiate the point and clarify the limits media can go to without it being termed as anti-national: "*In a democracy, the people have a right to know the why and wherefore of a national disaster. The government is accountable to the people. Where the government fails in its duty, a publicist may step in to fulfil that task.*"

Given the right understanding of each other; the relationship between the military and media could be further improved and strengthened. There is a typical Indian media environment that differs vastly to that of any others and there are different expectations, feelings and associations depending upon the regional character. Both, the military and media, have to make conscious efforts to minimise frictions if any and maximise the comparative smoothness. What Arthur Lubow says is true that in modern war, reporters must be permitted in the war zone, and they must submit to sensible censorship. Mutual mistrust is a part of the shared heritage of soldiers and journalists in times of war. So is mutual accommodation.[72]

References

1. Leena Parmar, "Kargil War and the Mass Media", *Armed Forces and the International Diversities* (Jaipur: Pointer Publishers, 1992), p. 319.

2. Rajdeep Sardesai in a television programme on NDTV 24 × 7 Channel on 8 June 2003, while in a debate on introduction of CAS in India with Minister of Information and Broadcasting and Ms Shiela Dixit quoted this figure.
3. N Bhaskara Rao, Opportunities and Challenges, *Vidura* (January-March 2003), p. 35.
4. Sangeeta Saxena, a professional in this field, in conversation with the author.
5. Jyoti Raghavan, Book Review on *Media Ethics in Asia* (ed. Venkat Iyer), *Vidura* (October-December, 2002), p. 42.
6. *Ibid.*
7. A Baijal, CEO, Prasar Bharati, Seminar "Media Reporting on Security and National Interest and Need for Self Regulating Mechanism" at IIC, New Delhi on 21 February 2002.
8. Ramesh Narayan Swami, IAS, "National Information Policy", *NDC Papers* 3/97, p.10.
9. *Ibid*, p.14.
10. Arvind Kumar (ed), *Encyclopaedia of Mass Media and Communications*, Vol. IV (New Delhi : Anmol, 1998), p. 13.
11. n. 5.
12. Vinod Mehta of *Outlook*, in the Seminar "Media Reporting on Security and National Interests and Need for Self Regulating Mechanism" held at India International Centre, New Delhi.
13. n. 5.
14. n. 10, p. 142.
15. VC Natarajan, "Media and Services – Need for More Interaction", *Trishul*, Vol. VI, No. 2 (January 1994), p. 81.
16. n. 10, p. 148.
17. Sangeeta Saxena, *Defence Journalism in India* (New Delhi: Manas, 1997), p. 24.
18. Manoj Joshi, *India Today*, Seminar "Media Reporting on Security and National Interest and Need for Self Regulating Mechanism" at IIC, New Delhi.
19. Maj Gen Winant Sidle (Retd), US Army, "Testimony Before the US Senate Committee on Governmental Affairs", in Hedrick Smith (ed), *The Media and the Gulf War: The Press and Democracy in Wartime* (US, Washington: Seven Locks Press 1992), p. 110.

20. "Role of Media", *Jammu and Kashmir Study Report*, USI (March 2003), pp. 79-80.

21. Malcolm Browne, "Testimony Before the US Senate Committee on Governmental Affairs", in Hedrick Smith n. 19, p. 141.

22. n. 10, p. 153.

23. AG Noorani, "The Defence Services and the Media", *Trishul*, Vol. IV, No. 2 (December 1991), p. 85.

24. Both issues are addressed in great detail in a book by Morrison and Tumbler of 1988 on *Journalism and War Reporting*.

25. Air Vice Mshl Kapil Kak (Retd), while replying to a question in the Seminar on Media and National Security held at IIMC, New Delhi, 27-28 September 2000.

26. n. 17, p. 12.

27. Dinesh Kumar, "Soldiers and Scribblers- Media in Information Warfare: A Case Study of India", *Occasional Paper Series*, *IDSA* (June 2001), p. 19.

28. *Ibid*, p. 6.

29. *Ibid.*

30. VC Natarajan and AK Chakraborty *Defence Reporting in India: The Communication Gap* (NOIDA: Trishul, 1995).

31. n. 27, pp. 6-7.

32. SC Bhatt, *Media: Sensation not Truth* (New Delhi: Gyan Publishing House, 2003), p. 55.

33. n. 18

34. KK Katyal, Minutes of the Seminar on 'Media and National Security' held at IIMC, New Delhi, 27-28 September 2000, p 46.

35. AK Sachdev, "Media Related Lessons from Kargil", *Strategic Analysis* (January 2000), p. 1799.

36. Sqn Ldr Rana Chinna (Retd), CAFHR, at USI of India, New Delhi.

37. JN Dixit, "Field Marshal Cariappa Memorial Lecture 1997", *Sainik Samachar*, 1-15 March 1998, pp. 3-4.

38. A K Sachdev, n. 35, p. 1800.

39. *Ibid.*

40. Lt Gen Harbakhsh Singh (Retd), *War Despatches: Indo-Pak Conflict*, (New Delhi: Lancer International, 1991), p. 209.

41. N Bhaskara Rao, *Indo-Pak Conflict, Controlled Mass Communication in Interstate Relations,* (New Delhi: S Chand, 1965), p. 1.
42. n. 37.
43. See the Appendix on '*Problems Faced by the Media during 1971 Operations*'.
44. n. 27, p. 21.
45. n. 35, p. 1800.
46 Author was himself present in Sri Lanka for two years during *Operation Pawan.*
47. Lt Gen SC Sardeshpande (Retd), as quoted in Dinesh Kumar, n. 27, p. 21.
48. Jean Dreze, "Information, Democracy and the Military Establishment", *Vidura* (October-December 2002), p. 11.
49. *Ibid.*
50. *Newsweek* Magazine, 8 October, 2001.
51. Amitabh Matoo, "Mass Media in South Asia", *The Book Review,* Volume XXVI, No 1, January 2002 (New Delhi: Chandra Chari), p. 42.
52. *Times of India*, 12 October 2001.
53. VS Gupta, "Covering the War in Iraq", *Vidura* (April-June 2003), p. 26.
54. *Ibid.*
55. Kieth Flory, *The Pioneer*, in conversation with the author.
56. n. 53.
57. n. 20, p. 79.
58. Lloyd J Matthews (ed), *Newsmen and National Defense: Is Conflict Inevitable?,* (New York: Brassey's, 1991).
59. Margaret H. Belknap, "The CNN Effect: Strategic Enabler or Operational Risk?" *Parameters* (Autumn 2002), p. 112.
60. n. 55.
61. "Tarnished Brass: Wither our Military Ethos?", *The Statesman*, 15 March 2002.
62. n. 20, pp. 82-83.
63. n. 23, p. 80.
64. USI Seminar on 'The Military and the Media'.
65. *Ibid.*

66. n. 23, p. 80.

67. BG Verghese, Centre for Policy Research, New Delhi, in conversation with the author on 01 March 2002.

68. n. 55.

69. Anonymus, as quoted in "Lessons of Media in Indo-Pak War in 1971" Please read the appendix at the end of the book.

70. General K Sundarji (Retd), "Media and National Security", *Trishul,* Vol. IV, No. 1 (July 1991), p.35.

71. Rajdeep Sardesai, "Vitual Diplomacy; Don't Shoot the Messenger", *Indian Express,* 25 July, 2001.

72. Arthur Lubow, "Read Some About It", The Media and the Gulf War: The Press and Democracy in Wartime", in Hedrick Smith n. 19, p.100.

4

Kargil : The Military and The Media

Kargil conflict has been covered extensively during and after it was over. The process of analysis, however, is still far from over. Several lessons have emerged from Kargil but confining it to the context of the subject of our study, the issue of the Fourth Estate as a force multiplier for the Indian Army still merits ruminating over. Lieutenant General Krishan Pal, General Officer Commanding (GOC), 15 Corps, responsible for the conduct of the Operations in Kargil, equated it with a roller-coaster ride with its own highs and lows while commenting upon the love-hate relationship between the Army and the media.[1] The Pakistani intrusion in Kargil caught the country off guard and confusion prevailed as to the true identity and the exact strength of the intruders. Initially, it was felt that it was the handywork of some militants, as Pakistan had intended the world to believe. Soon analysis gave rise to a more correct and factual assessment of the situation.

Media had a small presence in Kashmir, reporting as they were on the gradual low ebb of militancy in the Valley and the oncoming high tide of tourism after a gap of nine years. A local Indian Airlines travel agent in Badami Bagh Cantonment area in Srinagar, remarked that in the last nine years he had not got as much booking on the flights in and out of Srinagar as he had got in the previous one month.[2] Things looked up for the Kashmiris in the month of May 1999 till the papers like *The Tribune* of Chandigarh published the first reports about the infiltration of regular Pakistani soldiers in depth areas of Kargil around 06 May 1999.[3] The paper attributed it to a local source in that area. Small and insignificant information such as this one, however, managed to attract the media. Initially, the news was not perceived as grave as it turned out to be. Some of the national level media men, who were present locally, did rush to

Kargil to confirm the details of the infiltration along with the regional press reporters. Not only the intelligence agencies but also the Army, the people and the nation itself seem to have been caught off guard when the enormity of the intrusion was perceived. There were many speculations about the true identity and the numbers of the intruders. Clarifications, assurances and denials started to emerge in the news columns. As the media started to descend onto the Badami Bagh Cantonment in Srinagar, the gravity of the situation began to unfold. Initially neither the Army nor the media were adequately geared for managing and regulating the flow of information for an event of this magnitude.

Restrictions on Media

Initially a trickle and later a torrent of the media started to flow towards the Headquarters at Srinagar to proceed to the affected areas. Initially, some doubts prevailed regarding the safety of media if allowed to go and report from the battle-zone directly. It might be worth mentioning here itself that visit of the media to any frontline posts requires a prior notice and clearance, even during peacetime.

In the beginning, the entry of media personnel into the battle zone came under a ban as per *Frontline* Bureau Chief Praveen Swami.[4] He entered the area on 19 May, breaking official travel restrictions. From 25 May to 04 June, journalists were formally allowed in. A ban on the entry and movement of the media in the war zone was once again placed on 04 June till it was finally lifted on 09 June.[5]

The contradiction suggests that some confusion prevailed at the handling stage at lower level in the early days of the battle about the entry of the media to Kargil area. Even when the alleged ban was lifted, the media was allowed access to the region only in hired civilian buses from Srinagar to Kargil and back with briefing en route. But what was objectionable, according to Dinesh Kumar, to the media at large covering the war, was the arbitrary issuance of special 'Passes' by the newly appointed Major General (at the ALC) allowing select journalists to hire private taxis and travel as they desired in the war zone.[6] Journalists in general were also critical of the fact that some of them were later permitted to fly by the Army helicopters. All this did not deter the determined lot of journalists to hire private taxis and slip through the traffic check posts at Zojila and other places. Some of the journalists flew to Leh by Indian Airlines and entered the war zone from that avenue as well.

As discussed earlier, the Army is a hierarchical organisation with a highly centralised command and control structure. It is also well known that the media operates at both the field and central levels. When the field staff in media contacts the Army in the field, military staff needs to clarify about it and seek approval from the higher authorities in chain, which takes some time. Needless to say that till the sanction is received no interaction is permitted. The authorities' oscillation between 'yes' and 'no' suggests the same dilemma.

It may also be noted that simultaneous contact by the journalists at multiple levels does have its advantages for journalists but it poses problems for military as there may always be certain changes in a developing situation not yet known upwards or downwards. These differences between various levels may altogether alter the perceptions of a third person who may not have the knowledge of the overall picture. More often than not, this is the main problem in such a situation. While the tactical picture at the ground level may be very clear, the strategic view or the thought would only be available at the higher headquarters. Therefore, it must be very clear as to who at what level in the Army may be contacted by a journalist and for what kind of information.

It is pertinent to add here that a well thought out and co-ordinated policy for any such requirements is the need of the hour but with a caveat that no permission will carte blanche be granted for every future requirement. Each case, where national security is involved, will have to be dealt with its own merits.

Sequence of events that followed in the early days of Kargil, the initial response by the authorities and the analysis offered by the media are contextually as important for analysis as any other matter and are reviewed hereinafter.

Initial Issues in the Media

The moment tremors from Kargil were felt in Delhi, the first, inevitable, reaction was to get the assessment of the senior Army commanders of the situation. The Chief of the Army Staff was away on an official visit to Poland. GOC, 15 Corps too was not available locally and was away. He, however, made himself available to tackle the situation on 07 May. The situation was unfolding at a very fast pace and was not endearing. The Defence Minister made a visit to Siachen on 12 May and on his way back to Delhi visited Srinagar on 14 May. Clamour to know the details resulted in a Press briefing on 19 May 1999 by the GOC, 15 Corps. A relevant extract of the briefing is reproduced below:-

"... 15 Corps did not undertake any press briefing in the interest of on going operations against the ISI and the Pakistani Army backed infiltrators in the Dras-Kargil sector. In order to put to rest all unnecessary speculation and propaganda by vested interest I have taken this opportunity to personally interact with you all this morning. There has been some infiltration in Dras-Kargil sector in completely unheld area on the Line of Control by Pakistan Army. These unheld areas are quite extensive and total up to 200 km in extent from Gurez Sector in the valley to Turtok Sector in Ladakh region. This infiltration is fully backed by Pakistan Army and ISI. Extent, magnitude, methodology, operational and logistic support to this infiltration clearly establishes Pakistan Army's and ISI planning, execution and subsequent efforts to sustain this operation. Primary aim of this infiltration is to revive the defeated proxy war and internationalise the situation by building up war hysteria. This is a local situation and would be defeated by us locally. There is no possibility of it's escalation into war. We are quite aware of the ISI and Pakistan Army's designs and would not fall into this kind of trap ..."

"... Our response to this infiltration has been very swift, well focused and hard hitting. It has resulted in taking away the initiative from them at an operational level. Infiltrators have been blocked, contained and cut off. Efforts to completely encircle them are continuing. They are being tackled peace meal. Due to difficult nature of terrain operations are time consuming ..."[7]

This Press conference did clarify a few things. However, it also resulted in a criticism about command perceptions. Talking about the intrusion as reproduced above, the Corps Commander had said that the intrusion was of 'local nature' and would be dealt with accordingly.

However, the reporters present misunderstood the term 'local' and they sent out an impression that the problem was of a local origin and local infiltrators were present and by implication that it was too insignificant. Whereas, speaking strictly in Army's phraseology what the General had meant, as per him, was that the problem was 'sector specific' and would be solved from the resources available within the sector.[8] Critics call this statement as an afterthought. Yet another remark by him (GOC, 15 Corps) in an interview found him in the eye of the storm. Talking about the intruders, he had said; *"If I don't take notice of them it will make no difference. If they come off the heights in the summer, they will be slaughtered. And if they don't; leave them in the winter, they will freeze to death."*[9]

To some of the critics in the media, this was a clear indication that the military leadership believed the intrusion at that stage to be little more than a localised nuisance, an abortive enterprise to push in irregulars into an area of Jammu and Kashmir until then unaffected by insurgent activity.[10] Events unfolded later; the National Highway 1A(NH1A) was under complete domination of these intruders; and not infiltrators in small numbers and this needed to be opened for the normal and military traffic. An early eviction of these intruders thus became mandatory.

As a matter of fact, media has put question marks on the assessment of intruders as given out by the Corps Commander and does not seem to have exonerated him of the charges made earlier. Some of the opinions are reproduced below:-

"Commander 15 Corps, Srinagar, thought it was nothing but an infiltration till his Officers and men began returning in coffins wrapped in the tri-colour."[11] **The Pioneer**

"Farooq Abdullah was the first one to call the infiltrators 'Pakistani Regulars' but Krishan Pal insisted that the situation was local and that it would be defeated locally. His assessment was totally contrary to the situation on the ground."[12] **A Soldier's Diary**

What is evident is the witch hunting[13] that went on immediately after the discovery of intrusion in Kargil. Every one wanted to know who was responsible for the intrusion and what was being done and how? Thus, the focus of the arc lights of media shifted on the Commander of the affected Corps. Every thing that he said was seen with the microscopic eye and any loopholes or lacunae were recorded, played and replayed time and again. The story refuses to die down even now. Another question often asked is that could we have won the Kargil War with much lesser casualties?[14] Divakar, a journalist, and so many others feel that substantial casualties occurred during the early days of the war, when the ill-prepared troops were rushed in to evict the intrusion. Divakar claims that, *"Having erred on anticipating and preventing the intrusion from taking place, senior commanders in charge of the operation sought to underplay the intrusion (probably to avoid getting the sack) while simultaneously trying to evict in great haste the intruders irrespective of the cost of the human lives."*[15]

However, what must be added here is that assessment of the strength; the exact location of the intruders and the nature of intrusion require deliberations before one can give a correct assessment. Firstly, a large number of inputs are required to confirm and reconfirm for which confirmatory reconnaissance by foot and air is done. Inputs are taken from the troops in contact (while here hardly any troops were in contact with the intruders at that time) and the assessment of the lower commanders is obtained. Even satellite photographs are taken and interpreted. It is a deliberate process that takes some time. To blame the Corps Commander at this early stage for not knowing the exact strength of intruders was perhaps not fair.

Media does exert psychological pressure on the commanders. Any hasty move or statement that is made the media obviously latches on to it and plays and replays it until it loses its sheen. If one were to believe every word in print and presume that these were all correct,[16] the moot question still remains; was the timing to ask such questions right? The timing of questions has a direct effect on the conduct of operations while exerting psychological pressure upon the commander being questioned. Therefore, a fear of vested party influence on the conduct of operations exists which could be catastrophic in the overall interest of the nation. A cue may be taken from the latest war in Iraq, where any such criticism of the senior military commanders was not to be seen or heard in the media during the war; post war it is now being analysed.

As one can make out, there are three distinct phases of media reporting; the first one being the *'objective reporting'* till a national crisis, such as a war or conflict, emerges. What is but natural is the *'nationalistic or the patriotic reporting'* once the battle lines are drawn and forces are at grips. Finally, the *'investigative or post-mortem reporting'* phase comes when the discovery of the truth is sought to be achieved. As far as Kargil is concerned, we have entered the last and final phase of the media reporting. A large number of books have come out and have been critical of many issues. Media did start the investigative phase a bit early during the battle itself and that is why the question of timings as discussed earlier. What is evident from the kind of media reports and analysis now is that investigative phase has begun and where it finally leads you to is not yet known. The media has been unable to sustain this phase due to lack of expertise on defence matters.

Barry Zorthian's observation on the Gulf War, before the US Senate Committee on Governmental Affairs, is relevant here *"...the military system of collection of information distilled for bare-bones presentation to the press is not designed to meet the media's desire for personal observation and for detail on the human element. At the same time, the journalist's approach is not a substitute for official evaluation and analysis. The two compliment each other and both are necessary to provide the public with the well-rounded basis it should have to form a judgement."*[17]

Media Briefings

A large number of journalists had lodged themselves in the scanty comfort of the only reasonable hotel called " Siachen" in Kargil during the battle. The day's rough draft of story was available through soldiers astride the NH1A, but to interact with someone to authenticate it, required time; both with the journalist as well as the army-brass, as the latter was busy conducting and directing his battle. Of course, at times there were delays in giving details where a clearance was required from the higher headquarters for want of safety of own troops and security of own operational plans. One such story that needed prior clearance had nearly brought Pakistani artillery fire on to own troops while the other story, a live coverage of final attack on Tiger Hill had nearly compromised the most essential part of any battle. The Corps Commander mentioned that it was to our good luck that Pakistanis didn't probably believe that the drama unfolding on TV screens was for real[18] and it resulted in the assaulting troops still managing to achieve total surprise and reach the top of Tiger Hill.

While it is not denied that for a journalist the time is of essence and is always at premium to meet his deadline, he was often besotted with the lack of availability of phone lines that were scarce in Kargil. Video tapes of Kargil stories were more often then not sent through couriers in trucks heading towards Srinagar, where the same would be flown by flights to Delhi. Unlike the war against terrorism in Afghanistan, videophones were hardly visible with any journalist, while only a few of them seemed to possess own satellite phones or laptops to file the story in time. They primarily depended upon the land phones for making STD calls, which was a rare commodity in the remote township of Kargil. Of course, some of the STD booths were opened post haste for troops to call up their homes. Journalists too used these phones-lines in an emergency in Dras and Kargil. On the other hand, some journalists gave their own satellite phones to the soldiers to make calls to their homes.[19] As we have seen in the war in Afghanistan, and now in Iraq, communications may not be a problem to the journalists in future. Accessibility to a senior military commander, to brief them on the war situation, may still persist till a solution of the inherent requirements and an effective medium in terms of local public relations officers are made available.

The Gulf War coverage by the international media and the enhanced understanding of the role of media, both, resulted in a need for a new way of briefing at the apex level during Kargil conflict. An update, given initially twice daily, on the war efforts and once later on, was available to the media to obtain the latest situation without going to all the places on the battlefield. Of course, reporters on ground supplemented the need for first hand reporting. A common man thus had the version as given out by the armed forces and also through the Radio, TV, and the print media, which was often accompanied by comments of the experts in the field.

Initially, the briefing was conducted at South Block by senior rank officers of the Directorate General of Military Operations (DGMO) and the Air Force. Later on, it was shifted to National Information Centre and expanded to include a spokesperson of the Ministry of External Affairs (MEA) of the rank of a Joint Secretary (External Publicity). Questions have, however, been raised about the media briefings on basically a military operation being presided over by an official from the MEA and also about the rank structure [20] of the Army officers who conducted the briefings.[21] It must be added here that an integrated approach is always better than the fragmented one; a holistic picture emerges with this method. So far as the rank structure is concerned, it may not be out of place to mention here that let an appropriate man do this job regardless of his rank and status. After all, to pull out one of the senior officers from the DGMO would amount to denuding one of the principal staff officers of the directorate, who at this juncture is perhaps most required to do his assigned job. Additional rushing of an individual who already has his hands full, would result in his parent task being handled by someone else. This may dilute his prime operational duties. There is a case here for a dedicated decision making level officer being available at such briefings, who in turn is assisted by an officer from the required field at the time of briefing.

Army Liaison Cell (ALC) and DPR

Kargil battle saw introduction of what has now come to be known as ALC under the Directorate General of Military Intelligence (DGMI). Earlier, it was known as MI 24 and was mainly responsible for psychological operations (PSYOPS). Major General Arjun Ray, with a previous experience in Kashmir was hand picked from the Army Training Command to head the ALC with a newly created appointment of Additional Director General (Media and Information). He was assisted by similarly experienced officers including the defence correspondent of the *Indian Express,* Manvendra Singh, who had put on uniform as a Captain of the Territorial Army and had desired to go to the battlefield.[22] Being an intra-Army department, it was felt that decision making would be quicker as it had little or no interaction with the MoD's civilian bureaucracy and would have better access to information being a part of MI directorate. Also, it would serve as a fast-track channel for the media to obtain instant access to senior officers for information, as also to obtain permission to visit military locations, such as in Kashmir or in forward areas along the LoC or the Line of Actual Control (LAC).[23] Evidently, the ALC was created to improve the interaction with the media.[24]

As the battle in Kargil joined in, three Media-Access-Nerve-Centres (MANC) emerged in the foreground; the existing Army PRO in DPR, the newly created directorate of 'Media and Information' and the Army PRO at Headquarters 15 Corps at Srinagar. In addition, there was a daily briefing given by the Military Operations (MO) Directorate. Some critics in media have often dubbed this as an unsatisfactory arrangement that delivered a cross-purpose briefing and often worked in conflict.[25] On the other hand, some of the critics have questioned the wisdom of last minute creation of an additional MANC as the DPR in the South Block had been functioning under Mr Swagat Ghosh with a well-established media-PRO working relationship.[26] Entry of the ALC brought in a new change in this working environment. Here onwards, most of the media related issues were handled by the ALC till the end of the battle when visit of the media to Kargil was organised by the Army PRO in DPR.

Hotel Siachen at Kargil town became the focal point where one could see journalists of all hues and milieu staying together and even surprisingly comparing notes, forgetting their professional rivalries. Every journalist who went to Kargil to cover the battle had a different story to tell; some of them were appreciative of the co-operation extended to them by Army authorities while others had a bag full of criticism. Dinesh Kumar believes that in this system, the directorate of 'Media and Information' became supreme and, in the process, also arbitrary.[27] Similar views have been expressed by Ajai K Rai when he mentions that, "*The role of the DPR, which functions under the MOD, was marginalised, and it had to be content with just providing administrative support for the coverage of the operations. No press party was taken by the MOD during the entire operations. The first conducted press party was taken only on July 21 and the second on July 23.*"[28]

What could be said is that in the absence of one agency dealing with the media, and the lack of an established media policy, an early fog in the environment existed which lifted shortly thereafter. As the battle became more intense so did the media coverage. Going into the details of the successful coverage of the battle in Kargil, one is bound to ponder whether this could be the result of the efforts of only some of the players concerned. Was it the media alone that did it or was there a deft handling at the other end of the continuum too? Introspection would give the answer to all these questions. Dangers of being ad hoc in the thick of the battle are well known but certain calculated risks too are warranted.

Balance in Media Coverage

Dras area is adjacent to the national highway. However, to reach Batalik a deliberate effort is required, as it is located away from the highway. Similarly, Turtok was out of the way. Although, the entire battle in Kargil has been covered during and after the battle, both, by the media as well as by the critics in the form of articles and books, it may be pertinent to evaluate whether there was a balance in the coverage of battle or not. A balanced coverage results in a harmonious development and shaping up of the battlefield environment. The balance in reportage of Kargil battle had shifted in favour of actions in Dras. Batalik and Turtok remained in the background despite most of the men in media wanting to go there. The imbalance happened for various reasons. One of the reasons was the Army pickets en route to Batalik. Ajai K Rai, laments the inaccessibility to Batalik. *"The road leading to it had four army pickets. Under orders of higher echelons, army employed its resources in intercepting journalists rather than Pakistanis. Even if you crossed one, there was not a chance in hell you could cross the other three. Journalists tried twice but failed."*[29]

Undoubtedly, if the restrictions were placed as alleged, these were unfortunate, as it did not give the desired transparency needed for the Army authorities. What must be added here is the fact that Batalik and Turtok continued to remain neglected even after the tempo of battle had picked up there. The reason of neglect is not attributable to the alleged restrictions alone; it had other possible reasons as well. One of them was the treacherous and desolate road without embankment going through a height of 13,500 feet leading to Batalik. Similarly, Turtok had a very difficult approach. Unlike the road through Zojila, the landscape had nothing to offer in case of an emergency. For a reporter, it was difficult to reach Batalik or Turtok, cover an event and return to Kargil or Leh by the same evening and file a report in due time. There was no level ground to pitch a tent anywhere in sight around Batalik/Turtok or en route should anyone dared to venture.

Another important reason to avoid Batalik and Turtok perhaps was that actions in Dras were along the NH 1A and were visible from the road. Thus, the battle could be shown on a day-to-day basis on electronic media/TV. The conduct of battle in Batalik and Turtok tended to concentrate deep inside the intrusion area, which remained largely out of reach to the journalists. Only the successes in Batalik or Turtok were published occasionally. This media approach had its own fall out. After all, the men in Batalik or Turtok were from the same stock as in Dras and needed a shot in their arms to boost their morale, and nothing like hearing their names on the radio or watching themselves on the television or reading about their exploits in the newspapers. Lieutenant General Bammi (Retd) agrees with this view when he says; *"As the media could not reach 70 and 102 Infantry Brigades, there was a feeling among these troops that their deeds were not fully highlighted or glorified."*[30] He further adds that *"Commander, 70 Infantry Brigade with eight units under command, had captured maximum territory; evicted enemy first from the 35 km frontage and accounted for the first (and six out of eight) Prisoners of War."*[31]

The size of intrusion and number of fortified peaks recaptured in Batalik were large[32] as were their other achievements; that included reaching the LoC earliest;[33] inflicting maximum casualties upon the enemy[34] and capturing more than fifty per cent of their arms and ammunition during Kargil[35] with comparatively lesser casualties to own troops.[36] Almost 11 battalions worth of troops were finally involved in evicting the intruder in and around Batalik, which is sizeable for any brigade headquarters to control,[37] that too with a greater degree of difficulty in Batalik and higher altitude and remoteness i.e. two to three days ahead of the road head.[38]

As seen from the above, comparatively difficult sectors, Batalik and Turtok, too, witnessed spectacular actions. What may be added here is that this possibly is an area where the media could really have acted as a force multiplier. While the media did it in Dras, it remained distant to Batalik or Turtok. Not that there was a dearth of sizeable matter-for-reportage as is clear from above but for some unknown reason it happened. How do we then explain the imbalance in coverage? Perhaps it was a combination of all the factors in varying proportions we have so far discussed. Due to lack of adequate media exposure, the finer achievements in these areas have gone largely unnoticed. A lesson for the media as well as Army is to evenly balance their reportage and the briefings respectively.

We will now look at some of the other issues figured in media. An analysis of the content and its repercussions on the policy makers in Delhi, the defence forces and on the conduct of operations in Kargil and the people in the country and abroad remain important topics for any case study of this nature. Almost all the issues touched upon by the media during and after Kargil are clubbed under various heads and summarised in the succeeding paragraphs, in a random manner, and not in any order or priority or merit. Although, scores of examples could be quoted to support an argument, yet to prevent verbosity, only limited examples have been given here. To cover the electronic media, generalised comments have been offered, as it may not be humanly feasible and practical to accurately report each and every one of them.

Kargil Commanders

One of the noticeable trends in media about Kargil battle is the praise of the junior officers, criticism of the senior officers and apathy towards the middle ranking senior officers. Intrusion in Kargil had taken place in two different brigade sectors. Media, however, focussed mostly on Kargil brigade and particularly wrote back about the inefficiency of Kargil brigade commander to keep vigil on the LoC. The Brigadier went on his defensive and was later replaced. A series of allegations and speculations became a norm in the Press in general and in *Outlook*, a weekly magazine, in particular. Speculative reporting to suggest rolling of heads of many other senior officers hogged the headlines. Fingers had been pointing towards other functionaries as well, *The Asian Age* had this to say: "*Military sources said the investigation will also examine the ineptness of Major General V.S. Badhwar, General Officer Commanding 3 Infantry Division based at Kargil and his operational Deputy Colonel (GS) Avtar Singh, in realising the extent and intensity of the intrusion several weeks after it was first discovered in early May.*"[39]

Undoubtedly, any lapse on part of any officer on national security matters is a cause of very serious concern and is unpardonable but before declaring anyone guilty, he must be afforded ample opportunities to present his case. The media is not a judge but a medium that should report only the facts and the truth. Unfortunately, select media went in to argue in favour or against some individuals. Their efforts made some of them look guilty of charges while others landed up being projected as innocent or victims of circumstances. It was too early to attempt a verdict; what it apparently resembled was a mere sensationalism. In hindsight, what can be said is that the media, which did such negative reporting and sensationalising of certain cases, could have been more responsible and not try to legislate and fan the fire.

While the senior leadership bore the brunt of wrath and fury of the nation through the media, the same media commended the junior officers and trusted them in whatever they had said. Undoubtedly, the credit for the success in Kargil goes to these junior officers; however, to discredit all senior ranking officers is worrisome. To borrow a phrase, what concerns the military is that it might lead to *the inverse credibility of the rank* [40] in which a junior rank officer is trusted more and the experienced senior rank officer is taken otherwise. The media needs to understand that while the junior officers fight the battles, the senior officers plan and fight the wars at macro levels. Officers' actions and results take place at fast forward acceleration, while macro matters move at deliberate slow speed replays.

The military and media both need to understand the modalities of war at these levels as today's junior officer is an aspiring senior officer of tomorrow and if he looses the image of senior ranking officers, an end to his aspirations will come sooner than later.

Lieutenant General Satish Nambiar (Retd), in the context of media taking their day's story from junior officers exclusively, commented *"Officers and other ranks at lower levels, will never be aware of the total perspective, and hence their observations could convey a distorted version of real larger story. In such cases, the media would be better advised to restrict themselves to human interest stories, and get the overall perspective from qualified persons at the appropriate headquarters."*[41]

Was the senior military leadership really poor as it was made out to be by the media? Was the media qualified to make these remarks? Our reporters were young, high on language, and low on operational and battlefield functional aspects.

Failure of Intelligence

In terms of intruders coming from across the border, history seemed to be repeating itself. Pakistan has done it earlier in Kashmir and it seems to be one of their pet strategies. Notwithstanding this, India once again was taken by surprise, this time by the presence of intruders in Kargil one fine day in early May 1999. Uproar in the Parliament followed the disclosure of intrusion in the news. What were the Army or the other intelligence agencies doing, is a question often asked but without any satisfactory explanation in sight. Were there any indications; were the clues ignored or did the people entrusted with this task sleep on their jobs? Entire media went on an overdrive with all such possible questions and rightly so, as the people in one of the largest democracies in the world deserved to know. Media had all such questions thrown in every where, and why not; as it is the media that is expected to be functioning as the watchdog of the nation. Rita Manchanda has a long list of such questions in her article "Covering Kargil: South Asia's First Media War".[42] Accusations and allegations on various military commanders and speculative suggestions for their removal were also made.[43] So strong was the wave to enquire that even if any one was doing any thing else during the battle, he was misunderstood as conducting some kind of discreet inquiry into the intelligence debacle. An article in *The Asian Age*, 20 July 1999, serves as a good example; "*A senior Colonel from the Counter-Insurgency School at Khrew near Awantipur in southern Kashmir has been given the task of investigating into events that led to the overall failure by General Krishan Pal's 15 Corps at Srinagar in detecting the Pakistani intrusion.*"[44]

Vikram Jit Singh, in his article, "Army for Secret Probe into Kargil 'Bungle'- not Many Soldiers Confident that Action will be Taken for Failure to Detect Intrusion" published in *Indian Express* on 21 July 1999, also expressed similar sentiments. He also quoted a Brigadier deployed in Kargil battlefield, saying thus: "*The scope of the probe embraces not only the factors that led to the intrusion going undetected but also the intelligence and operational failures in the first few weeks of the battle.*"

What may be added here is that serious efforts are always made by journalists to first ascertain all the facts before publishing a story. However, at times, speculations or hearsay do find their way in media. Credibility alone is not in question here, what is more serious is the sustenance of the war effort that gets affected by such reports and hence a special care has to be taken in such matters.

The potency of the media was in full display. The Kargil Review Committee was ordered and it submitted the report in record time with its findings. Notwithstanding the failure of the intelligence, we need to analyse as to what in the media would act as a force multiplier and expedite our reaching the objective earliest. Here, we must once again take a cue from the Americans and their media. With all kinds of sophisticated technology, the intelligence failed to gauge the resentment against the Americans in some parts of the world and the result was a tragic loss of so many lives in the 11 September 2001 attacks. But despite this historical intelligence failure, the American media did not raise a hue and cry to demand any resignations. The media instead strengthened the hands of President Bush to deal with it firmly and worked in unison with the government to report subsequent events with a refrain. Maturity lies in handling a situation correctly and calmly in adversity and wait for the right time and opportunity to act. In case of the intelligence failure in Kargil, may be we could raise the issue immediately and definitely, but had waited to tighten the screws on until each and every Pakistani was evicted from Kargil. Immediate reporting and demanding the sacking of concerned individuals runs the risk of fanning the frustrated desires of certain disgruntled elements who may take advantage of the situation. Such reportage goes contrary to the accepted belief in the force multiplication effects of the media as there is a time to question and also there is the time to be supportive to the cause of the event. Freedom of expression is a right and that too a fundamental one, but along with every right comes the responsibility; and in a case such as this one, it was to see the impact on the frontline soldiers and commanders that any of the reports is likely to have.

Lack of Equipment, Acclimatisation and Casualties

Many years ago, John Masters, the novelist who had served in India, was commissioned to write an appraisal of the Indian Army. His verdict: "*The Indian Army is a force with first-rate men, second-rate officers and third-rate equipment.*" Much of Masters' assessment about the equipment remains true to this day,[45] although the situation is slowly changing now. The media highlighted the lack of snow clothing to the soldiers fighting on the icy heights of the Himalayas. The shortage of boots, proper winter clothing, surveillance devices, modern rifles and gun radars were some of the glaring inadequacies reported in the media.[46] General VP Malik, the Army Chief went on TV and bemoaned the lack of modern equipment for his troops. He decided to fight "with what we have".[47]

The soldiers deserve better arms and equipment when fighting under difficult conditions and all efforts must be made to equip them best for the job they are required to do. 3000 pairs of boots and much more for the frontrunners were airlifted.[48] Part of the credit must be given to the media for bringing about this much needed respite through reportage. Lack of gun locating radar did result in own casualties, as own artillery could not locate enemy guns to counter enemy bombardments. A major percentage of own casualties were due to enemy shelling. Unlike Kargil, the issue was highlighted a bit too late, as the efforts of the Army to procure the equipment had been a matter in existence for quite some time without any fruitful results for want of adequacy of funds.

Purchase of ammunition for Bofors guns too was brought to notice by the reports in the media. What is creditworthy for media is that the expediency and dire need to procure ammunition and equipment, such as these, was well understood by the authorities after the expose.

Why must we, including the media, only wake up to the call of bugles in the war zone? Prior to or post Kargil, media has once again forgotten the soldier and their legitimate and professional needs and the focus shifts back only when something sensational has happened. Continuity in reporting is one of the key principles on which media gains the number of loyal eyeballs or readership, if it is ignored then it has its own cost.

Acclimatisation and Casualties

Process of acclimatisation was followed in the employment of troops arriving immediately after the initial wave of one or two battalions as against the initial media reports. Initial battalions, unfortunately, had to be launched without waiting for the acclimatisation due to the expediency of the situation. However, what must be added here is that their tenure in the

Valley had partly trained and acclimatised them to face such eventualities in high altitudes. It may be worth recalling that some of the battalions launched immediately in Batalik were those who had returned from Siachen Glacier and were fully acclimatised to operate in high altitudes. However, the physical strength of men present was nearly half and their battalion support weapons were not with them. Subsequently, the planning period to launch the battalions during the initial stages did act as an abridged acclimatisation for the troops moving in from Kashmir.[49] An analysis of the wounds inflicted and published as an Annexure *A Ridge Too Far* by Captain Amrinder Singh does give a figure of 793 casualties due to High Altitude Pulmonary Oedema, Hypothermia and cold injuries during the period between 3 May to August 1999 by sourcing it to Major General Jaswant Singh, AVSM (Retd), Consultant Surgeon to the Army.[50] This figure, however, does not give a complete idea about the casualties, and requires further examination and comparison with normal period and other similar sectors before arriving at any conclusions. An independent analysis of the weather related casualties will have to be undertaken to benefit from our experiences in Kargil.

It must be mentioned here that there were some speculations in the media about the Army deliberately quoting lower casualty figures.[51] However, in an ethical question of grant of benefits to the affected families of the soldiers, a case such as this is unthinkable in the Indian Army.

On the other hand, Pakistan Army did not bother to collect their dead bodies or own up their casualties - an issue well known by now. It must be granted to the Indian Army that the figures were correct and no fudging was ever done. It was clearly visible to the glare of the media, where each an every dead body arrived in his respective home town to a funeral fit for a martyr. Credit is largely attributed to the media in general and the television in particular who brought the nation nearer to the near and dear ones of those who had lost their lives by filming the body bags arriving back home. It inculcated a spirit of involvement of the entire nation. One of the articles by Rita Manchanda had this to say: *"Every state, waited to claim its Kargil martyr, whipping up a mass patriotic hysteria, reinforced daily through endless footage on television. A wave of nationalist resurgence swelled around these martyrs as television trailed them to their homes in Kerala, Nagaland, Punjab, Rajasthan and Orissa, mapping out a heroic India and heroic Indians."*[52]

Vacated Posts and Intrusion

Winter vacation of Posts tactically not important, all along the LoC, right up to Siachen, has been the practice followed by the Army on our side. Reasons for this were either the Post was not viable administratively during the period of excessive snow or that the area was impossible to reach during that period. The Army claimed that there was no Post vacated if it merited to be held physically and only one of its 25 winter posts in the South West Spur of Point 5299 in the Kaksar sector, popularly known as Bajrang post, was vacated after a heavy snowfall in March 1999.[53] Due to the large area all along the Line of Control, large unoccupied gaps existed not only on our side but also on the other side of the LoC. The area astride the LoC beyond Chorbatla to almost South of Siachen was one such example where both the sides were not held due to extremely difficult terrain.[54] 'Bajrang Post' in the Kaksar area was one of the posts that came under media glare besides the large gaps, which were surreptitiously occupied by the intruders.[55] Usually, such gaps or vacated Posts were regularly patrolled by the units in the vicinity to ascertain any violations of the LoC. The focus, however, seemed to have drifted towards countering the insurgency in this area. With the number of troops remaining the same, the effect of concurrent dual tasking was evident on the LoC. What finally emerged was a laxity in not having ensured compliance of the existing instructions, which resulted in loss of lives of our brave soldiers.[56] Kargil Review Committee's inquiry into this matter points out the same failure.[57] Claims made by the media, such as Marpo La and Sando Posts had no presence of troops during winters, however, are unfounded and not true.[58]

Frequent reports in the media and other publications by various researchers have indicated Pak intrusion details in Kargil sector. A summary of the details gives the enormity of the situation Indian troops had to face. The intrusion in Mashkoh Valley was right up to Point 4875, which dominated the National Highway 1 A. Similarly, in Dras sector, right from the Highway the entire Tiger Hill and the Tololing features, right up to the LoC, were occupied by the intruders. Kaksar area had the intruders perched atop many features such as Bajrang Post and others, a mere few kilometres away from the main road. Batalik area comprised of Jubar, Kukarthang, Khalubar and Padma Go ranges, which were completely held by Pakistani troops. Attempts of intrusion in Chorbatla (Batalik) were foiled by the Indian Army and was reported by the media.[59] Sub Sector Hanif, a sector renamed after Lieutenant Hanifuddin,[60] too was occupied by the intruders from Pakistan and an attempt was made to subvert the locals in Turtok area.[61] If we measure the physical length and breadth of entire intrusion area, it works out to be approximately 180 kilometres and the depth of intrusion ranges anything up to eight to ten kilometres. Exact details of number of Posts, especially behind the Posts closer to the Highway and right up to the LoC, were not available to the media for obvious reasons. However, various other publications on Kargil amply bring out these details in their true perspective. Nonetheless, media account of recapture of all these Posts faithfully reinforces the above summary. Therefore, it would be imperative to qualitatively and quantitatively analyse the media reports.

Recapture of Posts

One of the foreign correspondents in Batalik, who had served in his Army (one of the elite Armies in the world today) earlier, commented that no other Army in the world would venture into a feat such as this one and be as successful as the Indian Army in ultra high altitudes.[62] After the initial setbacks, the Army got its acts together and Tololing (Dras) was attacked on 12 June 1999.. After very gallant actions including hand-to-hand fighting that lasted over a few days, the soldiers were able to capture this complete feature.[63] This was the first turning point. After that Point 5140 (Dras) on 20 June; Point 5203 (Batalik) on 21 June; Three Pimples (Dras) on 29 June; and Jubar OP (Batalik) were captured. The second turning point in the battle came with the capture of Tiger Hill on 4 July 1999.[64] Scores of accounts of these recaptures were splashed or highlighted in the media during the course of the battle and well after it was over.

Stories of acts of sheer bravery of young soldiers and the officers created scores of heroes who became legends in the Army and icons of selflessness and bravery in the eyes of common men. Media portrayal of the battle was so powerful that the nation united like never before. It truly influenced the masses from the Himalayas to the shores of Indian ocean, from Hari in Meerut to Harry in Mexico, from a man in the streets of a metro city to the remote villages of the north east, from a rich man in a high rise building to a pauper in the slums, from the film stars in Mumbai to the common Rikshaw-puller who offered a free ride to any one connected with Kargil. This overwhelming support to the battle in Kargil translated itself into an overwhelming desire to throw the enemy out of Kargil. The valour on the front in Kargil was the source of inspiration and the Fourth Estate was the medium through which it travelled and touched the inner souls of the masses, thus, forcefully coming out as a force multiplier for the Army.

Notwithstanding the acceptance of media's role as a force multiplier, some critics, however, have questioned the neutering of the adversarial role of media in the name of bolstering the morale of fighting men.[65] Some of the other questions asked are :—

- What about the media's role in questioning–why is it necessary for these men to die?
- What about the role of the media for establishing accountability?
- Should journalists be patriots first and reporters second?[66]

Answers to all these questions are not easy and have been attempted by people concerned from time to time. A few of the questions have also been discussed in this chapter subsequently.

Capture of Pak held Posts was covered by the media with as much accuracy as possible under the constraints of not being allowed to move with the fighting troops.[67] Road-head-journalism was a new term that was heard during this battle and media remained constrained to stick to it.[68] Although, media was ever willing to go as far ahead and right up to the LoC, for want of their safety and also security of own troops and plans, they were not allowed to be with fighting troops. One of the dangers of interacting with the troops available after an event had taken place, is that it allows time for an individual to reconstruct the actual story according to his perception. Thus, there is a need to allow media's presence as far ahead as possible. Another danger that the men in the media may guard against is interaction with those who are termed as LoBs (Left out of Battle) in the military jargon. The Army on their part must allow the media to be with the fighting troops and preferably with the integrated unit as was done in the Second World War[69] and, more recently, in the War in Iraq.

Crossing of Line of Control

During Kargil battle, one of the terms of reference given to the Army as well as to the Air Force by the government was to not cross the LoC, thus, putting serious limitations on the impending operations by the Army and the strike capability of the Air Force. Given a situation like it was during the initial days of the battle in Kargil, the Army possibly had these options to clear the enemy from those heights:—

(a) Conduct operations close to the National Highway 1 A, first, to clear the enemy so as to open the road for normal traffic and thereafter go sequentially to capture heights one after another till the LoC, thus, rolling up the enemy positions.

(b) Go stealthily behind the enemy and first capture posts in his rear astride the LoC, thus, strangulating him and clearing him downhill later.

(c) A combination of both the above options along with going across the LoC to destroy his vital administrative or communication hubs such as his headquarters locally as well as opening another front.

Against the last option an argument was made that the prospect of the international community's support dissipating the moment India is seen as 'escalating' the conflict, was higher.[70] As a result, the other two options, the first option in Dras and Mashkoh and the second one in Batalik were utilised. New terms were coined for these two options; while Dras strategy was termed as the 'attrition approach', the approach in Batalik was the 'manoeuvre approach'. One of the Military Operations Directorate Press releases (for Batalik Sector) had this to say; *"The enemy defences in Batalik Sector have crumbled owing to the relentless pressure maintained by our ground forces and the heavy attrition caused on the enemy coupled with administrative strangulation effected by our* ***encircling manoeuvres*** *(emphasis added), which resultantly dampened the enemy's will to fight."*

Pertinent question that merited further debates in the media was that could Kargil be fought in any other way and what would have been the implications? Was there merit in attacking upwards, starting from National Highway, or first infiltrate up to the LoC and choke the supply line of the intruders before attacking him from his rear? There was hardly any debate in the media on these issues. The point made here is to emphasise the power and the reach of media (both, physical and mental) and the contributions media could further make during the battle.

Some would however have preferred the last option of crossing the LoC.[71] Nevertheless, the point highlighted here is the disclosure made through the media about the assertion of not crossing the LoC by Indian troops. It is noteworthy that an ambivalent posturing about crossing the LoC would have kept Pakistan tied down to many other options and further facilitated our conduct of operations, perhaps at a lesser cost of lives. It does make sense to keep enemy on tenterhooks by holding out a credible threat?[72] It thus reiterates the point brought out earlier that your own intentions or plans must not be made clear to your enemy even inadvertently, and, the media has a very vital and important role to play in this matter.

Withdrawal of Intruders

Once the Pakistani defences crumbled in Batalik, Dras and Mashkoh and their designs convincingly defeated, Pakistani authorities decided to pull back from the areas of intrusion to ensure that their troops were not completely encircled, leading to surrender or annihilation by the onslaught of the Indian Army. Pakistani Director General of Military Operations (DGMO) used the 'Hotline' on 09 July proposing a pull out in a phased manner. The two DGMOs met at Atari border on 11 July 1999 and reached an understanding. The historic meeting between the two DGMOs[73] was an event media had waited for, as it provided them with a bag full of stories. Mr George Fernandes, India's Defence Minister was quoted about grant of "Free Passage" to the withdrawing intruders and there were many such speculations in media, only to be clarified soon that the Minister had been mis-quoted.[74]

Withdrawal of Pakistani soldiers followed as a result of the political and military understanding. International media called it a product of arm twisting by the Clinton Government, while the media back home hailed it as the victory of diplomacy and military, combined. The mood in Pakistan was that of shock, as true revelations of the situation on the ground had emerged for the first time ever since the beginning of the conflict.

Media focus was shifting from one event to another in this fast developing situation. On one side was the Clinton-Nawaz meeting and its implications on international diplomacy while on the other was the fast crumbling of Pakistan held positions. As a result, justice done to the analysis of the tactical situation remained inadequate, as were the Indian Army's achievements.

In this moment of victory for India, media, however, skipped to note that Pakistan wanted to avoid the humiliation of her Army at the hands of the Indian Army and, hence, the clever move to opt for withdrawal in a hurry. Had there been no withdrawal for a couple of days more, Pakistani Army was once again facing a clear and decisive defeat after the 1971 debacle.

Before proceeding further let us recapitulate the chronology of events that took place in Kargil. We might recall, Chorbatla (Batalik) had been clear of intrusion ever since 31 May. In Dras sector, Tololing had been recaptured by 13 June. And thereafter, the forward movement of Indian soldiers on the ridgelines and mountaintops of Kargil became order of the day and Pak positions fell sequentially one after another.[75] Tiger Hill top was recaptured on 4 July and almost entire Dras was clear of Pakistani Army.

Similarly, in Batalik, Point 5203 had been recaptured as early as 21 June and Jubar fell on 29 June.[76] By 8 July, nearly 21 peaks on Jubar and Kukarthang ranges had been cleared in Batalik sector.[77] Troops had already reached the LoC in Batalik sector in an earlier timeframe. Incidentally, Military Operations Directorate, as per their Press Release (Batalik Sector) of 9 July had this to say: *"In some of the most spectacular operations carried out, 99 percent of the intrusion has been cleared of the enemy in the Batalik Sector. In this sector, the enemy had occupied four ridgelines, which have been cleared by the relentless offensive operations mounted by the ground troops...Presently in Batalik Sector, the enemy is holed up at only one position, which will be cleared at the earliest."*

Operations in Mashkoh Valley began after the fall of Tiger Hill and made steady progress. In the next few days, heavy fighting on Point 4875 resulted in recapture of this feature by 7 July and advance towards the LoC had begun here too.

Commenting on the overall situation General Malik had said that by the time Pakistan withdrew its troops, nearly seventy five per cent of the intruded area, including all high features dominating NH 1A highway had been retaken.[78] Basically, the balance twenty five per cent area that General Malik had in mind probably was Kaksar Sector and Sub Sector Hanif where, due to low priority, the operations had yet to begin in all earnest.

Indian troops were already on the LoC in Chorbatla (Batalik) and LoC had been reached at some other places in Dras and Batalik too. Steady movements towards the LoC in Mashkoh were on. It was a matter of time the complete and visible collapse of the remaining Pakistani held position was evident. Very soon the Pakistani Army would have been decisively defeated and pushed back beyond the LoC. Realising the gravity of the situation, Nawaz Sharif went to Washington to meet President Clinton on 4 July. Mian Nawaz ultimately gave in under US pressure. He had taken his wife along with him to never return back to Pakistan under a situation like this when his premiership was threatened by his own people (read Army) in case his decision was not acceptable to them. He was not confident yet he returned to Pakistan, perhaps at the behest of Americans.

To recreate events, let us presume that Nawaz Sharif would have discussed the matter with his Army Chief after he reached Pakistan, who in turn had to confer the same with his Corps Commanders before a decision was taken for the Army to withdraw from Kargil. Probably Musharraf, the Army Chief, had a conference on 7/8 July with his Corps Commanders.[79] Once the decision was taken, the first contact with Indian DGMO was made on 9 July on the 'Hotline' with a proposal to withdraw from Kargil.[80] Pakistan Army has an established command and control system and by no accounts it is likely that without any orders from their superiors the soldiers would start returning from Kargil on hearing the Clinton-Nawaz agreement of 4 July. There would have been some time gap before orders percolated down to the troops' level from their military commanders.

A deliberate look at the chronology of events as discussed above reflects that situation in Kargil for Pakistan, right from 29 June onwards, had become politically and militarily adverse. It was becoming worse each passing day. Tiger Hill in Dras, Point 4875 in Mashkoh, Peaks on Jubar, Kukarthang and Khalubar-Stangba ranges in Batalik crumbled mostly in this period extending up to 9 July and mopping up operations of the Indian Army were in progress.[81]

When the focus of the media shifted from the ongoing battle to Clinton-Nawaz meeting, due emphasis on the analysis of the ground situation in Kargil also started suffering. As a result, following impressions were generated: first, the withdrawal was misunderstood and credited to the US pressure on Pakistan. Second, recapture of peaks post 4 July became easier for the Indian Army and fell in quick succession due to the fact that different mindset had been created after the Clinton-Nawaz meeting. The first impression helped Americans to establish their credentials to broker peace in this sub-continent. The first and second impression, combined, helped Musharraf to honourably get out of the possible accusations of leading the Pakistani Army to her defeat; after all, it is well known that Musharraf was the 'chief architect of Kargil'. Net gain by accepting to withdraw led Pakistani Army to retain part of their honour and an acceptance of Musharraf as the Army Chief and later as the President of Pakistan.

A question comes to our minds – had the Indian Army been given a few days more before the so called understanding, the decisive defeat of Pak soldiers at the hands of Indian Army would have been more visible not only to the Indians but also to the entire world and more specifically to the Pakistanis; who still seem to be harbouring doubts about it. A question to ponder about is that had this defeat of Pakistani Army been given its due place by the media, could they (Pakistanis) still have backed up a defeated army's chief in all his successive manoeuvres to govern the country? Did lack of media exposure to this fact help General Musharraf to cover his weak underbelly where he was most vulnerable? Is this the reason that, unlike in India, no official account of Kargil War has yet been attempted in Pakistan? Wouldn't this account be a doctored version at that stage? Answer to all these questions would probably be the scope of research for another study on the subject.

The above analysis was aimed at providing a fuller perspective that remained comparatively lesser understood. Not only the course of the war but even the history of the region could have been different had the entire truth been analysed in the above context. A probe is still possible and the media could take the intended hint.

Picking up the thread from earlier paragraphs, let us see how far did Pakistan go as far as withdrawal was concerned. Pakistan breached the understanding by delaying the withdrawal and used this time to lay mines and extricate heavy stores and weapons. Pakistan also did not honour this political and military understanding to withdraw from these heights on our side, close to the LoC. The Indian Army had to launch attacks on these features from 23 to 25 July 1999.[82] The sanctity of the LoC was thus restored but at a later stage. However, certain speculations about Point 5353 in Dras Sector did dominate media headlines long after Kargil was over.

Bofors: Direct Shooting

Right from the early days of modern methods of fighting, Topkhana (artillery) has been used in the battlefield to support the foot soldiers' efforts on the ground. Kargil battle saw the emergence of artillery as the most important and potent tool to achieve victory. Bofors artillery guns, which had achieved notoriety in the past (for reasons other than their battlefield versatility), did wonders for the success of attacking troops in Kargil. *India Today,* in their 26 July 1999 issue said, *"The Bofors howitzer finally effaced its politicised past and became the sword arm of the Indian Army".*

Booming guns and precision shooting in an innovative manner was a sheer delight for not only the soldiers on ground but also the media and very specially the television viewers. The viewers at home saw the guns in action from the comforts of their drawing rooms. To be candid, this is as close as they (media) could go to the actual scene of the battle. Flashes of fire emanating from the barrels and exploding on the top of Tiger Hill and lighting up the sky is a scene people at home are not likely to forget in a hurry. Cameramen and journalists took tremendous risk of being present at every occasion the guns fired a salvo. Risk of enemy retaliatory counter bombardment at the gun end did not deter them to film the shot. There were a few journalists who even got injured in this process.

If the 1947 battles of Zojila revealed General Thimayya's tactical genius in deploying tanks on mountain heights, the 1999 battle of Kargil introduced the new tactical concept of using long-range heavy artillery in a direct-firing role in the hills.[83] Indeed, this concept (direct-firing by medium guns) was not visualised even by the makers of Bofors as commented by an officer trained abroad and commanding a Bofors Regiment during Kargil.[84]

It must, however, be remembered that due to the nature of terrain where the features like Tololing and Tiger Hill were visible from the roadside and the gun areas, direct shooting could be resorted to. This was not the case in Batalik as you could not take a direct shoot; the target is not visible from the gun areas in most of the cases.

Media paid glowing tributes to artillery by calling it a gunner's war. Kargil was a series of typical battles restricted to one part of the LoC. It was possible to concentrate an extraordinary weight of firepower both in number of guns and weight of shells leading to the evolution of 100-gun concept in fire support. However, a caveat must be added; the luxury of the 100-gun concept and limitless ammunition is unlikely to be repeated in a future conflict. Kargil was a special case where a handful of the Army and Air Force fought in a clearly demarcated and restricted theatre on our side of the LoC.[85] Lest we have similar expectations in a dissimilar future scenario, the Army and media both must not forget this lesson.

Air Campaign

The Indian Air Force began their Operations in Kargil on 26 May 1999 by pounding at Tololing with armed helicopters. The Army had bid for the air to start their campaign as early as 13 May. There was an urgent need to carry out reconnaissance along the affected line of control so as to ascertain the exact nature of intrusion and its details. The Indian Air Force's views were that the employment of air had to be completely packaged with air defence, attack helicopters and fighters and not the armed helicopters alone for close support of the battle as desired by the Army. Also, the use of air arm might escalate the situation and lead to an all out war with Pakistan as aircraft were likely to cross the LoC while delivering the bombs, for which political clearance was a must.[86] The decision to employ the Air Force was discussed in the Chiefs of Staff Committee without arriving at any results. The decision had to wait for the arrival of the Chief of the Army Staff from Poland. Finally, on 25 May a decision was taken to use the air arm for the battle in Kargil.[87] The period beginning with the loss of surprise by the intruders and the time co-ordinated action against them began left gaps which offered obvious advantage to the intruders.

Loss of two aircraft in Batalik sector and the resultant loss of Squadron Leader Ahuja's life and capture of Flight Lieutenant S Nachiketa by Pakistani forces as well as the loss of an armed helicopter in Dras were very well covered and reported by the media. On the other hand, the government in Pakistan literally used this opportunity to launch a propaganda campaign against India through the media. A large number of international media reporters were flown in to the air crash site in Pakistan Occupied Kashmir.[88] Nachiketa was shown on Pakistan Television. To the domestic audience in Pakistan it asserted moral ascendancy over India and the victory by Pakistan and for the international audience it tended to reflect India's aggressive designs. Media, thus, became a tool to conduct diplomacy at this juncture.

A new tactics was adopted by the Air Force to bomb enemy's dugouts in Kargil. The aircrafts were to fly at an altitude of nine kms above the affected area to avoid being hit by ground to air missiles. However, such an employment was not too accurate and there were reports that bombs fell either too far away from the objective or too close to own troops. A survey conducted by the author during this period reveals that troops on ground neither had the prior intimation nor the knowledge as to when and where the aircraft came and dropped bombs except initially at Tiger Hill and Tololing and, later, at Muntho Dhallo.[89] General Malik had this to say in an interview to *Sunday* magazine, *"Air strikes were not as effective against enemy posts but the IAF kept innovating and were ever willing"*

The Air Chief admitted that, *"No doubt that every attack was not a successful attack, if you miss the summit where they (intruders) are sitting, bombs and rockets would fall one or may be five kms away, depending on the rate at which the hills fall away whereas, in the plains, they might fall just 50 to 100 yards away from the target."*[90]

At a later stage, the use of some other ammunition, however, was a success story. By 12 July 1999, the IAF had flown approximately 580 strike missions, supported by around 460 air defence missions like Combat Air Patrol, Escorts, and about 160 reconnaissance sorties. Helicopters accounted for approximately 2,500 sorties transporting more than 800 troops, casualties and tons of loads besides flying scores of strike missions. Operation Safed Sagar was the first time the IAF fought a limited war, hitherto thought to be an unlikely eventuality, as air power and escalation to an all-out war were regarded as synonymous.[91] Air Commodore Jasjit Singh, former Director, IDSA has talked about the role of air power in conventional deterrence in a publication titled *Kargil 1999–Pakistan's Fourth War on Kashmir.* Major General Ashok Mehta on the other hand views fitting of Kargil on Gulf War and Kosovo template wrong as there was no adversarial air activity in Kargil.[92] Both these views are valid and each has its merits.

The point made in above paragraphs is to see the exact nature of the media coverage of the actions by the Air Force. As we have seen in the case of Gulf War, the support of ground operations by the Air Force is one of the most important operations of any war. If the reporting is not solely dependent upon the handouts or briefings and is done with painstaking efforts, corrective measures can be undertaken in time and loss of lives and wastage of time can be avoided, thus, adding to the war efforts. An impression of the IAF striking a correct rapport with the media is being perceived when a senior journalist remarks that, "*The IAF came out marginally better than the army. It held one background briefing for defence correspondents during the war followed by a major news conference towards the end. In the background briefing given by the operations directorate, the officers candidly confessed that in the initial days the IAF had not been successful in their strikes.*"[93] He goes on to add that the news conference held by one of the topmost IAF officers was more forthcoming on statistics and operational details. The Services must be more candid. While conducting background briefings one could furnish as much details as possible without compromising the safety and security of own troops and plans.

Role of the Navy

The Indian Navy played a very vital role during Kargil and it needs to be highlighted here that it had the desired impact on our adversaries. The Navy's role was to ensure that the conflict remained localised and did not escalate into a full-fledged war. Therefore, it went on full alert by 20 May. Strike elements of the Eastern Fleet were shifted to the North Arabian Sea and a major exercise Summerex West was conducted to flex our naval muscle. Pakistan's total dependence on imports by sea of its petroleum requirements through the port of Karachi was threatened. Anticipating disruption of their sea lines of supply and replenishment due to a blockade at sea by the Indian Navy, the Pakistan Navy started escorting oil carrying merchant ships to Karachi.[94]

The Navy extended its scene of action up to Gulf of Oman and missile firing, anti-submarine exercises and electronic warfare were carried out to step up pressure on Pakistan. Since the lone aircraft carrier INS Virat was undergoing repairs, the use of alternate platforms for operating Sea Harrier fighters, including large merchant ships was proven. Naval amphibious forces from the Andaman Islands to the western seaboard were also inducted.[95]

All these activities needed to be conveyed to Pakistan and her people and none other than the media was vital for this purpose. Media played its role, once again, as a true force multiplier by highlighting effective maritime activities. Pakistan understood the determination of India to vacate the intrusions at any cost. International maritime military analysts, and a lead story by the reputed *Janes Fighting Ships 2000-01* publication, have credited the Indian naval strategic manoeuvres during the Kargil conflict to be one of the two recent manoeuvres which have prevented the escalation of a potential volatile situation.[96]

Burial of Dead Bodies

India's media must be credited largely for this change in human face of our armed forces.Bodies of martyred soldiers were mostly flown out to the nearest place to their hometowns. Television channels showed coffins wrapped in the Tricolour arriving at the airports and last posts being sounded in presence of the defence and state authorities. Pictures of bereaved families putting up a brave front in the face of the calamity were everywhere to be seen. As Mr JN Dixit correctly observed, *"Another important decision, which resulted in high levels of intellectual and emotional backing for the government, was the decision to send back the bodies of the officers and jawans killed in Kargil to their homes in cities, towns and villages in different parts of India. It was the first time since Independence that the armed forces agreed to undertake this onerous responsibility. The physical and emotional impact of the bodies of the martyred soldiers in their hometowns and the last rites being performed with military honours in public ceremonies aroused public feelings."*[97] Undoubtedly the sending back of the bodies did have an emotional impact on public opinion.[98]

The surge of nationalism generated mainly by the portrayal of the Kargil battle by the media was such that even the militants in the North Eastern states of India decided to halt their activities against the armed forces to allow the soldiers to concentrate on the battle in Kargil. This mobilisation of public support and opinion transformed and galvanised the war effort and resulted in the astounding victory in Kargil. The factor common to all, upon which it all hinged, was the media; and if this factor could really multiply the war effort in a positive direction, imagine if it were to do the reverse, thus qualifying to be a strong and potent force.

A controversy did arise when one of the private airlines had problems in transporting the bodies of the soldiers for some reasons.[99] Financial aspects also had to be worked out as the bodies were sent for their last rites at state expense. One would dare say that every organisation, be it commercial or otherwise, has some social responsibility and for a cause like this expenses are far less comparable than to a possible few days strike. This reminder has also to be given and none but the media can do so.

In sharp contrast, Pakistan totally ignored her dead soldiers. Indian soldiers at the icy and rocky heights in Dras and Batalik cremated hundreds of Pakistani dead soldiers as per their last rites and with full military honours. Coverage of these cremations in most of the cases was adequately done not by the Indian media alone but also by the international media. Strictly speaking, the media coverage did show to the viewers across the border and the international community about the humane values upheld by India and her abiding to the international protocols and duties. Pakistan not only ignored her dead soldiers but also the captured prisoners of war. Once again the media played its role to the hilt in this context. Interviews and photos were in the news about these PoW.[100] But what shocked the nation most was the return of brutally mutilated bodies of Lieutenant Saurabh Kalia and other soldiers taken prisoners by Pakistanis in Kaksar earlier. Media, already in a state of overdrive, strove to gain further heights and projected the barbaric nature of Pakistani Army. A sense of total shock and outrage in the Indian minds followed the event; in fact the bitterness still lingers on. The media largely had an immense sense of nationalism but wherever anything came to their notice that was actually not in tune with the Indian philosophy and image they did not hesitate to publish that story either. An example, whether true or otherwise, was the media report of a head; the disembodied face of a slain soldier (Pak) nailed onto a tree, which was reportedly a gift for the Brigade at Dras (sic).[101]

Human Interest Stories

One of the best coverages of war by the media is one portraying not only the dark side of humanity but also the sensitivity, sensibility and sentiments of those involved, or even remotely related to it. Kargil battle coverage was no exception. We saw a large number of stories about soldiers writing home their last letters or receiving mail from a cross section of the society besides from their near and dear ones at home. The harsh living conditions of soldiers, the stuff they ate and the words they spoke were all there to be read and reread, seen again and again on the television screens, thus, transporting the readers or the viewers to the battle zone to be one with them. Words such as *"Yeh dil maange more"* spoken by Captain Ravi Batra, atop Point 5140 became headlines in a few newspapers. Not only what happened on the LoC was passed on to the masses at home but also what was happening on the home front reached the battle zone through the media. The distance between the front and the home thus blurred and afforded a unique kinship with the soldiers. This in turn led to boosting of morale of the men in uniform. The common man knew now about the life of the soldier on the battlefront. Maroof Raza, a TV personality and an ex army man himself, commented, *"Kargil was the watershed mark in the militarisation of the Indian mind."*[102] The stories of the deserted villages in Kargil area and the travails of the locals and their live stocks also found themselves as the lead stories, occasionally.[103] Migration of local populace to safer places in Zanskar valley and cattle roaming around in desolate villages, closing down of local schools and approaching winters without a good harvest, all triggered a civic action programme.

Media Omission

An important contribution made by Ladakh Buddhist Association (LBA) in Batalik area was not noted by the media and hence not highlighted. One may recall, there were civilian porters who were hired to carry loads in the war zone. However, the LBA decided to do this free of cost. Every able bodied person, whether he were a School Head Master or a casual labourer ferried loads in high altitudes right up to the LoC in turns and rotation.[104] Neither the booming guns nor the adverse weather conditions deterred them. They cheerfully, willingly and quietly did their perceived duty. Nation needs to know their names and faces and recognise their contributions. What more can be a better human-interest story? Media could well cover it now!

Media Patriotism

Some researchers have analysed the regional news coverage of the battle in Kargil and have been critical of the role played by the media that reinforced state perspective and prevented dissent. As per them the media could have been an effective counter point to the state promoted jingoistic patriotism; instead it showed little desire to initiate debate and discussions on the need to avoid war completely. Dipankar Sinha writes, *"As the 'war' gained intensity, the 'credibility curve' of the Indian media began to slide downwards. If at the end of the 'war' the BJP would euphorically describe the Indian media as a 'force multiplier par excellence' it was not an exaggerated estimate. The Indian media, including the two newspapers* under focus here, for various compulsions ranging from electoral-political to down right commercial, have served the cause of the state which by virtue of having monopoly over force, tends to project the military solution as the best possible solution. The media came to the state's aid during the 'war' by framing its news in such a way that for the readers the distinction between military achievements and patriotism blurred."*[105]

* The two vernacular newspapers examined were *Anand Bazar Patrika*, a privately owned newspaper, with the largest circulation in West Bengal, and *Gunashakti*, owned and controlled by the Communist Party of India–Marxist.

This view, as per him, was not to underestimate the dedication of soldiers who risked their life in 'war' but to draw attention to the way in which dedication of soldiers was manipulated by the media in reinforcing the statist perspective of militarised patriotism along with putting of moratorium on dissent.[106]

Free media, it must be remembered, is not a mouthpiece of the state and the government and it was true of the Indian media during the Kargil days. It can be said that if anything is represented by the media it is the popular sentiment of the masses. Certainly, the freedom media enjoys in India is a cause for envy for many journalists in other countries. Immediately after the Lahore process ended, the detection of intrusion in the Indian territory left no scope for any option other than the military one. Also, if we look at the international press or the electronic media coverage of the Gulf War or subsequent to that during the American war on terrorism in Afghanistan, we would note how the media offered a sanitised coverage. Commenting on the US media coverage of war on terrorism in Afghanistan, Siddharth Varadarajan had said, *"During more than 24 hours of news watching, this correspondent did not see a single studio guest questioning the legality, morality – or even utility – of the bombing."*[107]

Recent coverage of War on Iraq by the Western media is another example that further reinforces the above perceptions. What may further be added here is the ability of the media to analyse or criticise anything or everything internal but where ever external dynamics are involved and the security of the nation is concerned, a patriotic and nationalistic approach comes naturally.

Of course, the media must always keep a watch on every step that a government takes, but to advocate dissent for the sake of a debate alone is not always the right approach.

Another interesting feature that Dipankar Sinha noticed in Bengali Print Media was the 'Pan-Indian Syndrome' which he described as dissemination of message that the whole of India thinks and acts alike when it comes to teaching Pakistan a hard lesson.[108] He, subsequently, goes on to add that Kargil incidentally posed a crucial predicament for the Indian Muslims to affirm their loyalty to their country. He mentioned that, *"Several Islamic organisations, some displaying over-enthusiasm, began to issue statements calling the government of India to teach the 'rogue-state' Pakistan a lesson... The phenomenon can be attributed to media's self-imposed duty to let the country, presently witnessing the assertion of Hindutva forces, know that there are patriotic Muslims around. However, the media failed to take a notice of the fact that by this 'well-meaning' act the media might play into the hands of the Hindu fundamentalists."*[109]

Pan-Indian syndrome is not denied. However, to mention the assertion of Hindutva forces and media playing into the hands of Hindu fundamentalists may not be true across the board unless the observations were limited to the Bengali Print Media alone and that too deserves further analysis before making a comment. What needs assertion and understanding is the fact that Indian Muslims do not have to prove their patriotism every time there is a crisis, and Kargil was no exception.

Commercialisation of Kargil

Perhaps, one of negative fall-outs of the media portrayal of Kargil conflict was its commercialisation. It was indeed heart warming to see the Kargil heroes being immortalised by installing life size statues in street squares, but profit oriented ventures, concealed in a proposition to help out war widows were not only in bad taste but also should never be condoned. After all, one can not and, in fact, must refrain from making a fortune on the martyrdom of a soldier. Unfortunately, at times the mass media was misused by some with vested interests. Would the media like to expose some of them even now and ask them to be accountable to the nation, lest they repeat it?

War inevitably generates inflation. Demand for goods increase, supply become scarce, which at times provides a boost to the industry. New requirements crop up, providing new opportunities in different fields. World War II brought the aircraft, telephone, wireless and weapons industries into a higher gear, yet all this was not termed as commercialisation. But the use of names of Kargil martyrs to generate funds often sounded unpleasant to many a sensible ear.

The media has to be applauded for bringing the Forces closer to the civilian section of society, but it has to maintain a gap between throwing the prestige and self respect of the armed forces to winds by overdoing sacrifices and ensure a strengthening of the bonds of solidarity of the people of this country to its soldiers. What is required is a sense of esteem for the forces - not pity or sympathy. This emboldens them to face the elements of fate during war with inherent guts and courage.

War Widows

With the growing nationalistic sentiments that swept through not only the length and breadth of the country but also echoing across the globe amongst the non resident Indians, a positive development – to settle the war widows–was encouraged by the media. The cover story on war heroes "Tears Mingled with Pride" [110] is just one of the hundreds of illustrations on the role of electronic and print media which covered and followed this other but humane side of the story. Beginning with the caption "The Brave Men who Sacrificed Their Lives for the Country Have Stirred the Hearts of Millions", the story goes on to read, *"The intermittent but heart-rending wails disturb the most stoic of men huddled at Niloti's chaupal (a place where village men assemble daily). But not the 20-year-old woman who receives condolences from the wailing women flocking to her residence. Her eyes are dry and her voice firm. 'My husband has sacrificed his life for the country and I would dishonour his martyrdom by shedding tears'*, she says."[111]

Needless to add here that such reporting went a long way in inspiring the empathy with the unfortunate ones who lost their close relatives during the Kargil conflict. The result was a pride the nation took in looking after and supporting the widows.

For the rehabilitation of the injured soldiers 'Kargil Relief Funds' were initiated by many popular magazines like *India Today* and were followed up right till the end, in true letter and spirit. Media did not spare anyone who defaulted on this social cause, and one of the popular examples was the NDTV programme 'Reality Bytes' anchored by Barkha Dutt. One of the most touching episodes on this programme was on the difficulties faced in establishing a Petrol Pump by the father of a Kargil martyr; who was shamelessly asked by someone to give proof of the fact that he fathered his son (sic).

The media focus not only remained on Kargil widows but also veered towards the fight against odds for those widowed during the previous wars.[112] Stories of widows of 1965 war and their resolve to bring up their children single handed, and their life staying afloat despite sinking of their hopes along with the sinking of INS Khukri appeared in the media.[113] Media stories did touch the hearts of the people and shake their conscience and the recognition of social responsibility followed.

Empathising with the widows was fine but somewhere down the line, sometimes it crossed certain boundaries to become partisan, thus, forcing the already unfortunate ones to stick to certain public norms. Expression of grief is a personal choice but when one is forced to react in an imposed manner, grief compounds. While quoting a media report on a wailing wife who lost her husband within three months of her marriage and described as one 'lacking mental-balance', Dipankar Sinha very rightly remarks:–*"It is a typical instance of media framing 'forcing' the displacement of women from the private space of the home and from their 'private being' to face the harsh, 'duty-bound', 'masculine', public and non-domestic space of soldiers."*[114]

Conventional versus Nuclear War Debate

Some sections of the media called Kargil a result of the Indo-Pak nuclear parity after Pokhran tests in 1998 by India and in Chagai by Pakistan. According to them, commentators had warned that nuclear parity would neutralise India's superiority in conventional arms and could promote limited incursions designed to keep the Kashmir issue alive.[115] Ajit Bhattacharjea had opined in the *Outlook* magazine that the Pakistani planners could risk the operation because they knew that Prime Minister Vajpayee would hesitate to hit back elsewhere across the LoC or the international border in Punjab, as Lal Bahadur Shastri did in 1965. As per him, they (Pakistanis) were willing to gamble that Vajpayee would have to consider the risk of a nuclear confrontation that neither side could win and its international repercussions.[116]

While talking about the book; *Pakistan: Eye of the Storm* by Owen Bennett Jones, Sumit Ganguly, Professor of Asian Studies and Government at the University of Texas in Austin, says that, *"The most recent misadventure, the Kargil crisis of 1999, came about a year after the Indian and Pakistani nuclear tests. Jones provides the most cogent and revealing account of this crisis to date. He suggests that Pakistani military can be held almost solely responsible for this singularly ill-concieved adventure, which also brought the countries to the brink of war. The army high command,"* Jones reveals, *"had started planning the operation in about 1994 in an attempt to disrupt India's ability to supply its troops on the disputed Siachen Glacier. Indian artillery barrages that year interdicted Pakistani troop movements and thwarted the original invasion plans. But Pakistani generals were undeterred and decided to await a more propitious moment. This came after the 1998 nuclear tests; the army assumed that India would not expand its military operations for fear of provoking a nuclear exchange."*[117]

India, unlike in 1965, did not resort to prompt horizontal escalation in 1999; instead, it carefully limited the war to a particular arena and did not even attempt to cross the LoC into Pakistan territory after dislodging the Pakistani troops from its own land.[118] One of the principal reasons for the Indian restraint, as per Sumit Ganguly's book,[119] was the acute awareness of Indian defence officials that their adversary possessed nuclear weapons and would resort to their use if vital interests or assets were jeopardised.

General VP Malik commented upon deterrence as posed by the nuclear weapons versus the escalation of limited war to full-scale war. In his view, it was the threat of escalation to full-scale war generated by the activation of conventional forces on air, land and sea, which capped the conflict. As per him, a strategic space exists between the limited war and the nuclear exchange.[120]

Arguments presented here notwithstanding, all that India wanted was to evict the Pak intruders from its soil as early as possible without additional territorial designs on land belonging to Pakistan. India has never been an aggressor with a view to grab her neighbour's territory and also, as a rule, would never accept any foreign violation of its territory. Prevention of horizontal expansion of the battlefield perhaps was more in tune with this thought process and certainly not guided by the factor of nuclear deterrence as it was brought out to be or perceived in the West.

Media played an intangible but vital role in highlighting that it was Pakistan who violated the LoC and until the status quo was restored and all the intruders return from Kargil, the Indian response was justified. Diplomatic efforts were thus greatly strengthened. 'LoC', a phrase unheard before, started to be recognised as something akin to 'International Boundary' in the international diplomatic circles as well as in the minds of common men. What, however, must be noted here is that it was more of the international media which theorised the nuclear flash point or the South-Asia-on-a-brink-of-nuclear-war bogey than the media in the two affected countries.

References

1. Discussion with the author.
2. Remarks made by a travel agent, Badami Bagh, Srinagar to the author a few days before Kargil conflict began.
3. Ajai K Rai, "The Kargil Conflict and the Role of the Indian Media", *Delhi Papers 17* (New Delhi: IDSA, 2001), p. 30.
4. Praveen Swami, *Frontline*, 16 July 1999.
5. Ajai K Rai, n.3, p. 31.
6. Dinesh Kumar, *Soldiers and Scribblers: Media in Information Warfare: A Case Study of India,* IDSA Occasional Paper Series (June 2001), p. 28.
7. Transcript of GOC 15 Corps Press Conference on 19 May 1999 published by Lt Gen YM Bammi (Retd), *Kargil 1999: The Impregnable Conquered* (NOIDA: Gorkha Publishers, 2002), pp. A45-46.
8. In an interview with Lt Gen Krishan Pal immediately after the battle at Srinagar.
9. Parween Swami, "War in Kargil", *Frontline,* 18 June 1999.
10. Ajai K Rai, n. 3, p. 24.
11. "Grossly Unfair", editorial in *The Pioneer,* 2001., Also Leena Parmar, "Kargil War and the Mass Media", in her book *Armed Forces and the International Diversities* (Jaipur : Pointer Publishers, 2002), p. 319.
12. Harinder Baweja, *A Soldier's Diary. Kargil.*, A product of the *India Today* group (New Delhi : Books Today, 2000), p. 39.
13. Nitin A Gokhale and Murali Krishnan, "War and Witch Hunts", *Outlook,* 2 October 2000, pp. 38-48.
14. M Divakar, "A Story That Refuses to Die", *The Pioneer,* 10 August 2002.
15. *Ibid.*

16. In an interaction with the author,. he denied that any under-assessment was made by him and was vindicated by the events that followed.
17. Barry Zorthian, Statement Before the US Senate Committee on Governmental Affairs, 'The Media and the Gulf War: The Press and Democracy in Wartime', in Hedrick Smith(ed), *The Media and the Gulf War: The Press and Democracy in Wartime* (US, Washington: Seven Locks Press, 1992), p. 102.
18. Stated in a conversation with the author.
19. Rajdeep Sardesai, NDTV, New Delhi.
20. Initially a Maj Gen, then a Brig and later on a full Colonel briefed the media.
21. Ajai K Rai, n. 3, p. 37.
22. *Ibid*, p. 36.
23. Dinesh Kumar, n. 6, p. 25.
24. The former COAS, General Malik confirmed it to the author in a personal interaction.
25. Dinesh Kumar, n. 6, p. 27.
26. Keith Flory, *The Pioneer*, in conversation with the author.
27. Dinesh Kumar, n. 6, p. 27.
28. Ajai K Rai, n. 3, p. 39.
29. *Ibid*, p. 32.
30. Lt Gen YM Bammi (Retd), n.7, p. 507.
31. *Ibid*, p. 501.
32. Brig Gurmeet Kanwal, *Heroes of Kargil*, an Army HQ publication, p. 53; Col Anjan Mukherjee, *God of War* , p. 293.
33. Maj Gen A K Verma (Retd), - *Kargil: Blood on Snow* (Delhi: Manohar Publishers, 2002), p. 111.
34. Capt Amarinder Singh (Retd), *A Ridge Too Far : War in the Kargil Heights 1999* (Patiala : Motibagh Palace, 2001). Intelligence records on page 102 and attributed 60 per cent enemy casualties during Op Vijay to Batalik brigade.
35. Col Shruti Kant, "A Year After Kargil", *Sainik Samachar*, 1-15 October 2000, pp 5-6 and Brig Gurmeet Kanwal, n. 32, p. 53.
36. Col Shruti Kant, *Ibid*, pp. 5-6; and Capt Amarinder Singh, n. 34, p. 96, thus attributing to 25 per cent own casualties.

37. Col Shruti Kant. *Ibid*, pp. 5-6 and Capt Amarinder Singh, n. 34, p. 96.

38. Col Shruti Kant, *Ibid*, pp. 5-6; Maj Gen A K Verma (Retd), n. 33, pp. 107 and 115.

39. Rahul Bedi, "Army Orders Investigation into Early Kargil Mistakes", *The Asian Age*, 20 July 1999.

40. Brig DW Montgomery, British Army, "Exploiting the Power of the Media", *NDC Papers 1/98*.

41. Lt Gen Satish Nambiar (Retd), "Reporting Comes of Age", *Vidhura* (July-September 1999).

42. Rita Manchanda, "Covering Kargil: South Asia's First 'Media War' ", in Kanti Bajpai, Afsir Karim, Amitabh Mattoo (ed), *Kargil and After: Challenges for Indian Policy* (New Delhi: Har-Anand Publications, 2001), pp. 73-91.

43. See earlier remarks in previous paragraphs.

44. Senior Colonel referred to in this article is none other than the author himself, who was deputed by HQ , 15 Corps to carry out research on training aspects and record the battle account while it was still unfolding.

45. Leena Parmar, "Kargil War and the Mass Media", in her book *Armed Forces and the International Diversities* (Jaipur : Pointer Publishers, 2002), p. 325.

46. JG Nadkarni, "The Army Needs Modernisation", *The Indian Express*, 11 August 1999.

47. Leena Parmar, n. 45, p. 325.

48. Discussion and meeting with Brig (now Maj Gen) A Chopra, Brig General Staff at HQ, 15 Corps .

49. Meeting and discussions with Lt Gen Krishan Pal.

50. Capt Amarinder Singh (Retd), n. 34, p. 101.

51. Initial views on media.

52. Rita Manchanda, n. 42, p. 87.

53. *Findings, Report of the Kargil Review Committee: From Surprise to Reckoning*, Executive Summary (New Delhi : Government of India, 1999), p.7.

54. Lt Gen YM Bammi (Retd), n.7, p. 364.

55. *Ibid*, pp. 190-191.

56. *Ibid.*
57. *Ibid.*
58. Author's Battle Diary.
59. This summary is an extract of various publications on Kargil and includes the reports and maps published in various books on Kargil battle.
60. Lt Gen YM Bammi (Retd), n. 7, p. 367.
61. *Ibid*, p. 364.
62. One of the Staff Officers in the Brigade Headquaters in Batalik area narrated the same to the author.
63. General VP Malik (Retd), "Kargil : Where Defence Met Diplomacy", *The Indian Express*, 25 July 2002.
64. *Ibid.*
65. Rita Manchanda, n. 42, p. 74.
66. *Ibid.*
67. Lt Gen YM Bammi (Retd), n.7, pp. 502-506.
68. *Ibid*, p. 504.
69. Sqn Ldr RTS Chhina (Retd), CAFHR, USI of India, New Delhi.
70. Cover Story, *Outlook Magazine*, 12 July 1999.
71. Author's Battle Diary.
72. Brahma Chellaney, "A New Myth Called Victory", *The Hindustan Times*, 30 May 2000.
73 Indian DGMO was none other than the present Chief of the Army Staff.
74 Lt Gen YM Bammi (Retd), n. 7, p. 466.
75 General VP Malik (Retd), n. 63.
76. Rita Manchanda, n. 42.
77. This fact is supported by the research conducted by the author taking into account all the publications on Kargil and arriving at a total empirically.
78. General Malik, n. 63.
79. Anil Bhat, "India's Costly Vijay at Kargil", *The Pioneer*, 23 February 2002.
80. *Ibid.*
81. 'Mopping up' refers to the clearance of the remnants of enemy in the Army jargon.

82. Rita Manchanda, n. 42.
83. R Prasannan, "Gunslingers par Excellence", *The Week*, 20 February 2000.
84. Author's Battle Diary.
85. Maj Gen A K Mehta (Retd), "Kargil, Real and Imagined", *The Hindustan Times*, 30 April 2000.
86. Raj Chengappa, "Kargil War:Interview, Air Chief Marshal A Y Tipnis", *India Today*, 26 July 1999.
87. Discussion and meeting with Lt Gen Krishan Pal.
88. Coverage of the event by international media such as BBC etc.
89. Author's Battle Diary.
90. Ajai K Rai, n. 3, p. 85.
91. "The Nation Remembers", *The Hindustan Times*, 26 July 2000.
92. Maj Gen Ashok K Mehta (Retd), "Kargil in all its Latent Glory", *The Hindustan Times*, 20 February 2000.
93. Dinesh Kumar, n. 6, p. 30.
94. "OPERATION VIJAY : The Maritime Dimension : An Untold Story", *The Hindustan Times*, 26 July 2000.
95. *Ibid.*
96. *Ibid.*
97. JN Dixit, *India-Pakistan in War and Peace* (New Delhi: Books Today, 2002), p. 63.
98. *Ibid*, p. 76.
99. One of the Staff Officers (name not disclosed on request) confirmed that the reason given by the airline was loss of revenue and objection by some passengers.
100. All major news channels on TV, Radio, newspapers and magazines gave an extensive coverage to PoWs.
101. Barkha Dutt, "Kargil : A View from the Ground", in Kanti Bajpai, Afsir Karim, Amitabh Mattoo (ed), n. 42, p. 63.
102 Ajai K Rai, n.3, p. 53.
103 Major TV news channels in July-August 1999.
104 Author's Battle Diary.

105. Dipankar Sinha, "Kargil Episode in Bengali Print Media", *Economic and Political Weekly,* 6 July 2002, p. 2806.

106. *Ibid.*

107. Siddhartha Varadarajan, "US Media Offer Sanitised Coverage", *The Times of India,* 12 October 2001.

108. Dipankar Sinha, n.105.

109. *Ibid*, pp. 2806-7.

110. V Radhika, DV Jathar and Shiv Raj Routh, "Tears Mingled with Pride", *The Week*, 4 July 1999, pp. 40-43.

111. *Ibid*, p. 40.

112. *Ibid*, pp. 44-45.

113. *Ibid.*

114. Dipankar Sinha, n. 105, pp. 2807.

115. Ajit Bhattacharjea, "The Nuke's Blunted Edge", *Outlook,* 5 July 1999, p. 28.

116. *Ibid.*

117. Sumit Ganguly, "Pakistan's Slide into Misery", *Foreign Affairs* (November/ December, 2002), Vol. 81, No. 6, p. 158.

118. Sumit Ganguly, *Conflict Unending: India-Pakistan Tensions Since 1947* (New Delhi:Oxford University Press, 2002), p. 110.

119. A senior General quoted by Sumit Ganguly, in *Conflict Unending, Ibid*, p. 110.

120. The General's talk at the USI of India, New Delhi on Limited War.

5
Media in Pakistan

Print media in Pakistan is fairly well developed. It has a large circulation of English and Urdu national and regional newspapers and magazines. The Urdu Press in Pakistan is far more conservative. Interestingly, the English media is often criticised for being very liberal and pro-India.[1] Pakistan's broadcast media, specially the television, is not as extensive as it is in India. Other than the state controlled Pakistan TV, private TV channels have yet to invade the skyline of Pakistan. As a matter of fact, a large number of people in Pakistan tune in to mainly Zee TV and other TV networks for entertainment.[2] Mr Mushahid Hussain, the Information Minister of Pakistan (during the Kargil conflict) had this to add during an India-Pakistan media retreat at Nagarkot, Nepal, on 11-12 May 2002, "*One example of an Indian programme which is watched very widely among the educated people in Pakistan is BBC World's Question Time India, which is produced by NDTV. It often focuses on Kashmir and Pakistan–related issues. It is an instructive programme for the insight it gives into the thinking of the educated Indian middle class. In general, the kind of freedom in India and the diversity of its news reportage is appreciated in Pakistan. There is certain resonance because they feel that the truth is being told, truth operationally defined as the criticism of the officially certified truth on a particular issue.*"[3]

While the Indian media covered Kargil largely without being subjected to any kind of fear, fuss or favour; the media in Pakistan, specially the television, seemed not to be entirely free of the government censor and control. What was discussed or shown on the television is a testimony to this fact. Pakistanis did make use of the new versatile medium of Internet too as a tool to inform and influence the literate class in Pakistan and the people abroad. Some of the Pakistani hackers also tried to get into a cyber war by defacing the Indian Army's website on Kashmir. It could, therefore, not be wrong to presume that Pakistan used the entire spectrum of information warfare tools to supplement the battle efforts in Kargil.

On conducting an objective analysis, a few facts emerged from the debris of media reportage and critical examination of the events in Kargil. Pakistani media had created an image of victory over India all along. Whether it was deliberate or government sponsored or an act of media's patriotism cannot be ascertained at this moment. However, when the bubble did burst and the truth dawned upon the masses, the world seemed to have come crashing down for them especially after the Clinton-Nawaz agreement. One of the leading periodicals of Pakistan, *Newsline*, titled its cover story as "Diplomatic Fiasco: Pakistan's Failure on the Diplomatic Front Nullifies its Gains on the Battlefield".[4]

Kargil was precieved as another defeat at the hands of the victorious Indian Army that rubbed salt to their wounds of the 1971 defeat in Bangla Desh. Air Marshal Noor Khan, former Chief of Air Staff of Pakistan was quoted in *News* of 25 July 1999 as saying, *"Pakistan has continued to make similar mistakes (since 1947) and has not learnt any lesson from the blunders that its ruling cliques have been committing."* Lieutenant General K Matinuddin, former DG, Institute for Strategic Studies in Islamabad opined thus: *"Kargil is a fiasco that has brought us humiliation and isolated us in the world while eroding our credibility."*[5] He even exhorted Pakistan to admit that Kargil has been a complete disaster and failure. Ayaz Amir wrote in *Dawn* of 9 July 1999: *"That the Kargil adventure was ill-conceived, if not downright foolish, was becoming clear, albeit slowly, even to the congenitally blind and benighted. That consequently Pakistan swallowing its pride and not a few of its brave and gallant words, would sooner or later have to mount a retreat was also becoming clear. But that the climb down when it came would be so headlong and ill-judged, and that in the process it would leave in tatters the last shreds of national pride, should take even prophets of doom by surprise."*[6]

The real reason for Pakistan undertaking the Kargil misadventure may not be known in its entirety. What emerges, however, is that the plan was not a fresh idea. It was conceived more than a decade earlier, in 1987, when Zia-ul-Haq was at the helm of affairs. It was shelved because the foreign minister at that time, Lieutenant General Yakub Khan advised Zia-ul-Haq against it, outlining its military, political and diplomatic defects. The plan was revived in 1994 and again in 1997 when Pervez Musharaff was the GOC of the Corps that had to implement it. It was planned to be put into effect in 1998 but according to the Pakistani newspaper *Nawa-I-Waqt*, Jehangir Karamat, the then Pakistani Army Chief, was not willing to push it through and consequently lost his job. In October 1998, Prime Minister Nawaz Sharif appointed Pervez Musharraf as the new Army Chief and soon after directions were given to put the plan into effect.[7] For Nawaz Sharif the stakes were very high as it would elevate him to be hero in the eyes of Pakistanis; also, Pakistan would be able to avenge the defeat of 1971 War with India. The Siachen stalemate too bothered the Pakistan hierarchy and a venture like this, it was assumed would catapult their sagging image. The editorial in *Friday Times*, 30 July-5 August 1999 had, however, this to comment, "*The Kargil operation was put on the drawing board by competent military minds many years ago. 'Kargil' was presented as a 'doable' option when the time was ripe, partly as a military revenge for the loss of Siachen and partly as a political device to spur the Kashmiri Mujahideen towards greater sacrifice and heroism.*"

Not all the reporting in the press or on the net was based on facts or rationale. For instance another Pakistani view of the battle in Kargil represented in *JI Media Digest* article 'A Good Game at Kargil' stated, *Indian habit of biting the areas here and there and calling them Line of Actual Control or Actual Ground Position Line is a normal misconduct. According to India all issues are bilateral and because of this ground reality the UN Secretary General Mr Kofi Annan's offer to send his envoy was rejected by India. The request by the Prime Minister of Pakistan to Kofi Annan was neutralised. The American and British authorities also favour this gridded position: good for India....bad for humanity. BJP policy statement after their nuclear tests of 11 and 13 May 1998 was: 'We will take back that part of Kashmir that is under Pakistan's occupation: we do not covet anyone else's territory, but we have taken a vow to take back what is ours. The Congress Party made a mistake in letting Pakistan control a part of Kashmir. We will correct that.'*"[8]

This, apparently, supported the media dis-information campaign that it was India who had evil designs on the soil of Pakistan. Another fact, which emerges from the analysis of the media in Pakistan, is the denial of employment of Pakistan Army in Kargil. To put it in JN Dixit's words, "*In the initial stages, say up to the beginning of June, the Pakistani media was successful in convincing the Pakistani public that the military confrontation in Kargil was between indigenous Mujahideen and the Indian security forces. Pakistani public opinion swallowed the government propaganda hook, line and sinker. The media coverage and television discussions in Pakistan made assessment that India was facing the logical "comeuppance" of its obstinate stand on Kashmir. Also expressed was the view that perhaps the Pakistani Mujahideen campaign against India had entered its last and successful phase and would soon dislodge India from Jammu and Kashmir.*"[9]

Not only had Pakistan succeeded in misleading its own people, but also there were complex challenges thrown up for India to internationally prove her moral high ground; Mujahideens on one side and the might of the Indian Army, aided by the Indian Air Force, on the other. Pakistan, initially, successfully put up a disclaimer that it was not the Pakistan Army but Muslim militants or so called Mujahideens, who were involved in the Kargil intrusion. Only a few militants, it was emphasised, had infiltrated; it was strongly stated that it was not an intrusion by the Pakistan Army. Therefore, the Indians would not have the moral rights to cross the LoC or use the air power against them. If either of the two or both the options India undertakes, she would run the risk of escalating the war, not horizontally or vertically alone but carrying the war from conventional battle to a nuclear exchange. Rhetorics were used effectively through the media. Of course, eventually the battle remained confined to Kargil region alone, but for different reasons.

While the artillery fire was reverberating from either side of the LoC, the version put across by the Pakistani media initially narrated tales of how the Kashmiri Mujahideens were fighting successfully on the heights of Kargil. For a prolonged period, Pakistan did not even acknowledge and honour their dead soldiers. However, it is impossible to hide the truth and media in Pakistan played its righteous role. In an article, "Kargil – A

Strategic History" in *The Herald,* July 2000, a local leader Hussain Shah was quoted as saying thus: "*When I first heard on the Pakistani media that the Kargil war was being fought by the Mujahideen, I was shocked. My children were being killed, but the laurels went to Qazi Hussain Ahmed.*"

Further coverage had this to narrate, "*There are over 500 flags flying across the entire Northern Areas (POK), home to the Pakistan Army's high-altitude warriors. The tombs are those of heroes of Kargil who fought valiantly in a war that seems to have many losers but no winners. Behind each of these tombs lie tales of struggle and valour, of neglect and disavowal, and of betrayal and unfaithfulness. But a year down the lines, these tales still remain untold.*" The paper went on to add, "*True to their tradition of glorifying soldiers, the people of the area were loath to accept the government's claim that the militants had infiltrated deep into the Indian territory. For the residents of Ghizer, Hunza and Baltistan, the districts which supply the bulk of NLI's manpower, it was only the NLI soldiers who were involved in these heroic deeds.*"

Pakistan Army took special care to hide their casualties from the eyes of locals and mislead the media but of no avail. One of the subsequent media reports summed it all up:—"*Over the next month; some 105 dead bodies passed along the jeep track that leads up to Yasin, Punial and Ghizer valleys in the central Northern Areas. Similar traffic appeared in the valleys of Hunza, Nagar, Gilgit and Baltistan. Residents of the area claim that the NLI soldiers who accompanied the bodies took care to move them at night in order to avoid publicity. As a rule, only one soldier accompanied a dead body... there were no military honours at the funeral, no hoisting of national flag and no gun salutes...the government's decision not to publicise their martyrs at that stage apparently created a room for all kinds of politics in the area.*"[10]

The denial of use of Pakistan Army in this misadvanture undoubtedly caused a stir in Pakistan Occupied Kashmir as M Ilyas Khan in *The Herald* suggests. He calls it the oppressive and dismissive behaviour of the Pakistani authorities causing ever-increasing resentment in the populace of the POK.[11] Qusting Hussain Shah of Mutahidda Qaumi Party, he stated,

"We thought that our sacrifices in Kargil would persuade Islamabad to give us our rights, but they continue to keep us in bondage. If this situation continues, he warns, the fate of NA will be no different than that of Indian-held Kashmir."[12]

Trouble did break out in Skardu where militants of Al-Badar Mujahideen had started arriving in late May to act, according to locals, as decoys for the Kargil operation. A meeting that was called to diffuse the situation turned ugly when a Pakistani Army Captain of the ISI hurled threats at SP Skardu, Momin Shah, for unduly favouring the Skardu residents. Shah, a native of Hunza, slapped the Captain across his face.[13]

Having faced a troubled situation in POK, Pakistan could no more keep the truth hidden and was compelled to accept that it was the Northern Light Infantry (NLI) who were used during the operations in Kargil.[14] However, having officially integrated the NLI into their Army sometimes in September 1999, Pakistan believes that it can still spin yarns by calling the NLI, during the Kargil operations, as their paramilitary force such as the Border Security Force (BSF) of India.

If one were to compile all the media reports emanating from the Pakistani side ever since Kargil happened, Pakistan would emerge as a state which would only concede to facts inch by inch that too when she is forced to do so. The first deception was the statement that the intruders were only Mujahideens, that too Kashmiris. The second was that the Mujahideens were not under the control of the government of Pakistan. Thereafter, forced by the events at home and pressure and proof from abroad, Pakistan has accepted that the intruders were a mix of Mujahideens and the NLI. Finally, the last word is that the Mujahideens were only used as civilian porters. Thus, it seems that they habitually take advantage by creating confusion.

Analysis of media adequately brings out the fact that the intruders were fully equipped with all the weapons such as the missiles and artillery guns, which only an organised army can possess. Intruders were integrated into full-fledged army brigades and were commanded and officered by Pakistan Army; a fact borne out by the study of the military honours and awards.[15] Does it not clearly indicate the army's involvement? If there were militants alone in Kargil, where are the details of them? Answer to some of the questions are still awaited. A booklet, *Pakistan Army's Misadventure in Kargil*[16] answers some of these questions and calls them the sordid tale of an Army (Pakistani) caught in a cobweb of lies. The book in question clearly publishes printouts of the photocopies of captured Identity Cards of Pakistan Army soldiers, their personal photographs in army uniforms, insignias of their battalions, diaries and letters written by them while they were at Kargil heights etc. There (still) is an impression in Pakistan, in the Kashmir valley and even elsewhere that Kargil was not a military rout for Pakistan.[17]

Notwithstanding the political and diplomatic mileage that Pakistan tried to gain by choking the media, the power of media did force the government in Islamabad to pacify the simmering discontent in POK. It further strengthens the argument in favour of the media being a potent tool which cannot and must not be ignored. Whether one likes it or not, the media will be there. And, once it is there, it will report and what it reports will form the opinion of the public. The opinion of the public once having gathered momentum will dethrone the rulers whom they dislike and that is what had happened in Pakistan.

While the broadcast media, specially the TV, went on an overdrive in India, Pakistan did remain constricted to their official channels alone. Pakistanis did acknowledge the Indian media blitzkrieg and the immense benefits India derived from the defining moment or the experience of Kargil.[18] Ban on viewing Pakistan TV and on the website of *The Dawn* in the first week of the 'war' for alleged false propaganda imposed by India, however, did come up for a criticism. In today's world, there is more than one battlefield and any unnecessary blockade of news would be dangerous.[19] Pakistan did try to encash and project it as the failure of the Indians to face the truth shown on their TV.

One must not fail to see an important aspect of use of the media by Pakistan; and it was not Pakistani media but the Indian Media. One of the senior retired Indian diplomats Mr JN Dixit in his book, *India-Pakistan in War and Peace*, has highlighted Pakistani government carrying out a public relations exercise to use Indian journalists and political commentators to generate dissension in Indian policies.[20] But in overall terms, this Pakistani effort did not succeed. Whatever be the substance in the case, any and every government must take note of such things and take adequate measures to prevent any such misuse of the media by a third party concerned.

References

1. Rehana Hakim, "Media During Intense Conflict", *HIMAL* (June 2002), p.17.
2. Mr G Parthasarthy in a discussion with the author, March 2002.
3. "Cross Border Television", Round Table Discussion, Mr Mushahid Hussain's reply to a question, *Himal* (June 2002), p.18.
4. Air Cmde Jasjit Singh (Retd) (ed), "Post Script", in *Kargil 1999 : Pakistan's Fourth War for Kashmir* (New Delhi : Knowledge World, 1999), p. 251.
5. *News*, 25 July 1999.
6. n. 4, p. 250.
7. The Kargil War-May to July 1999, p. 81.
8. Downloaded from JI Media Digest website.
9. JN Dixit, *India-Pakistan in War and Peace* (New Delhi : Books Today, 2002), p. 74.
10. *The Herald* (Karachi), July 2000, pp. 26-27.
11. M Ilyas Khan, "Second-Class Citizens", *The Herald* (Pakistan), July 2000.
12. *Ibid.*
13. *The Herald*, July 2000, p.29.
14. Read the May 2002 Conference Report on Kargil Project on www.ccc.nps.navy.mil.
15. See the list of Pakistan's Kargil Heroes available on the net.
16. Copy available in Army Liaison Cell, Army HQs.
17. "Information as War" an editorial in *The Times of India* , 28 April 2000.
18. May 2002 Conference Report, n.14.
19. Dipankar Sinha, "Kargil Episode in Bengali Print Media", *Economic and Political Weekly*, 6 July 2002.
20. Himmat Singh Gill, "Incisive Account of Indo-Pak Ties", *The Tribune*. Also read J N Dixit's book, *India-Pakistan in War and Peace*, n. 9.

6

Conclusion

Change, continuity and balance are the laws of nature. A paradox, that the more things change the more they remain the same, is also true. Notwithstanding this, an effort must always be made to give a positive direction to a change. In the preceding chapters, a review of the existing ground realities besides analysing the Kargil battle had been motivated by the same objective. An effort was made to examine the relationship between the military and the media with a view to arrive at some conclusions. The traditional defensive military stance and apprehensions of the media, both need modification to provide a foundation of an improved relationship that would benefit both the parties. The analyses contained why the relationship has been defensive, what lies beneath the Olive Greens, what makes the Fourth Estate tick, what both parties want from each other, areas of common ground and the environment in which future relationship will have to work. The aim has not been to pass judgements on performances but to ensure that the Fourth Estate truly remains a force-multiplier. The case study of the battle in Kargil was to reach the contemporary platform and plunge into the future. What really emerges is the creation of a change in attitudes as the first and foremost requirement. Production of a media policy, organisational changes, provisioning of infrastructure and a broad education and training programme are just a few of the changes that may be suggested. We have to also constantly be on a lookout, and factor into our thinking and planning, the need for the demands of modern conflict with the changes as desired by the modern media. The study has thrown up certain features, some of which falsify a few popular perceptions while the others reinforce them. Before finalising any suggestions, one is compelled to summarise the findings.

Summary of Findings

(a) Prior to Kargil, adequate thought and preparations to handle and manage an event, such as a surprise and short military conflict like Kargil, had not existed. Both, the military and the media, were inadequately prepared to deal with this unexpected situation. Also, there was hardly any prior thought given to the media policy to cater for such a requirement. This fact is borne out by the requirement of frequently changing the policy to react to the emerging situation. Some of the changes we saw were the confusion and the initial restrictions on media, changes in media briefings, reintroduction of Army Liaison Cell (ALC), redundancy of Directorate of Public Relations (DPR) for most of the duration of the conflict and the policy on foreign media.

(b) Notwithstanding the initial restrictions, media sustained a flow of credible information from the battlefront to the masses back home. The initial restrictions, lack of integration of media and lack of establishment of well thought out media camps or the media access nerve centres resulted in some avoidable criticism and concentration of the media in one half of the battle zone. Batalik and Turtok sectors remained on a low priority for media coverage for various reasons and, as a result, many of the finer achievements in these sectors remained less appreciated.

(c) Central briefings of the media through TV was a major source of information and proved to be a well thought out innovation. On the battlefield, however, the media still had to look out for the latest briefs with limited gains. The reporters strung out all along the National Highway 1 A to obtain first hand account of the battle. Media was not permitted to accompany the soldiers in direct contact with the enemy and, thus, the battle accounts were those obtained from the people available at the roadside. Organised media visits to Tiger Hill or Tololing tops did very little to satisfy the ever news-hungry media. The media did not appreciate preferences given to foreign media and some of the major news channels.

(d) Little or no administrative infrastructure was available to media personnel in Kargil and they had to fend for themselves for their daily sustenance.

(e) Environment in the battle zone, however, was media friendly and a lot of bonhomie existed between the committed troops and men from the media.

(f) Coverage of the conflict was fairly comprehensive, transparent and indeed a pioneering effort. It went into a lot of credible details of the battlefield environment, conditions and progress of the Operations with stories of valour and bravery of men and, to an extent, criticism of failures when and to whom it was due. Plight of civilian population in Kargil was adequately covered and so were the other stories of human interest.

(g) Media coverage of Kargil included analysis of the battle where veteran and retired soldiers offered comments and analysed the battle. The analysis was apt, qualitative and empirical and acted as a stimulant to the course of events that followed. Greenhorn journalists meanwhile thrived on interesting and sensational stories.

(h) The coverage of the battle also included a few errors and mistakes that media undoubtedly will avoid in future. Live coverage of planned Operations - such as on Tiger Hill, giving exact location of troops and, thus, inviting enemy artillery to open up on our combatants; the disclosure of start of an attack, prematurely, indicate a lack of training/experience of media men as well as absence of clear directions to men in uniform responsible for allowing such a coverage.

(j) On the whole, media was offered reasonable amount of freedom to report whatever it wanted. Barring a few exceptions, most of the media reported in a very responsible manner. The reports filed by the journalists and the editorials published in newspapers and discussions held on the broadcast media – all of these were as transparent as they possibly could be. No traces of propaganda were visible and there was no media 'spin' either. On the contrary, transparency in the media went towards the other extreme. Possibility of crossing the LoC was firmly rejected by the government and reported very transparently in the media. An ambiguous stance reflected in the media possibly could have got better and quicker dividends.

Knowledge of our exact response better prepares the adversary to make things all the more difficult for us and, thus, affecting the course of the battle.

(k) Media was nationalistic in their approach towards reporting of the battle in Kargil. A true portrayal of the battle scenes not only enhanced media's credibility but also the understanding in the common public the need to have a potent and free competent media during such a time. The impact on the masses was a surge of patriotism and a feeling of being part of the battle—never witnessed before in recent history. Media, played an exemplary role in linking the forward troops to the common people and the Government back at home. With media's forward and backward sweep completed, morale of the soldiers skyrocketed and, undoubtedly, victory in Kargil followed despite many odds.

(l) Coverage of the battle by the Indian media outshone the efforts of the media from across the LoC. Although, repeated broadcasting of battle scenes by one of the popular Indian TV channels came in for some criticism from the Pakistani media yet, they lauded the role played by the Indian media. Pakistani media, on the other hand, did not seem to be as free in reporting as was the case in India. A large number of books on Kargil written by Indian media men and women, as against one so far by a Pakistani, are further testimony to this fact.

(m) Although, the ALC got resurrected at the nick of time for Kargil, it proved to be of immense value to media. However, it was not without some criticism as it made the DPR redundant for that duration. DPR on the other hand remained on a low key and almost non-functional until the end of the battle when visit of foreign media was organised by them. Value and usefulness of DPR cannot, however, be undermined, as it provides sustainability in the long run.

(n) Air operations were given a reasonable coverage and the Air Force public relations (PR) exercise was well appreciated by the media.

(o) Policy of the Government to ban Pakistan TV and website of

Dawn came in for a lot of flak. It is now felt that such a policy generally is counterproductive.

(p) The media lacked dedicated and seasoned war or defence correspondents. A large number of media personnel were of a younger age profile with little or no previous training of reporting on defence matters. However, the lack of training was more than compensated by their enthusiasm and zeal, as they could easily identify with and relate to the young officers and soldiers on the ground. Senior Officers' bashing and criticism was another hallmark of Kargil reportage and a serious introspection is the crying need of the hour.

(q) Radio has been the most indispensable item on a soldier's kit inventory in the border areas and during all the wars India has fought so far. It has once again proved to be the same during Kargil. It would not be an exaggeration if it is rated as one of the most important items with them, as it is their one and sole trusted link with people back home, with civilisation, from those icy heights.

(r) Media coverage of bringing the dead Heroes back home and plight of war-widows caught the attention of public and government alike. A criticism, that by showing the plight of war-widows media invaded their privacy, does not hold water.

(s) Kargil conflict, unfortunately, also offered a platform to some of the organisations to commercialise it.

SUGGESTIONS

Attitudinal Changes

The military as well as media need to change a few of their attitudinal perceptions of each other before an effective and useful flow of information takes place. Fortunately, what it requires is not a paradigm shift, as all it needs is the understanding of each other a little more. The all-pervasive presence of the media must be factored into the overall operational plans. It would be worth an idea if at each feasible level of command in the military there are trained, designated and authorised people who would not only interact with the media but would also cater to their daily personal, functional and professional needs in the battlefield. Accepting the reality of media presence and catering to the requirement would pre-empt many problems invariably and repeatedly faced by the media. The media may note that for the committed troops it is not simple to meet their needs at all times.

Rules and Regulations

Security of the impending operational plans and the safety of own troops are definitely important but a right balance has to be struck between sharing and withholding the information with the media. As an exception to the rule, it may become essential to take the media into confidence on occasions. Some background information must always be handy not only with the military but also with the media. A rational approach to declassification of what is mostly considered confidential or secret must be undertaken and implemented. Much has already been said about the Official Secrets Act, 1923 and suitable modifications to it will obviously improve the environment. Also, a revision of the applicable paragraphs in the Regulations for the Army will need to be undertaken expeditiously. Media on their part need to have a control mechanism to prevent breach of security. It may be advisable to frame a strict code to avoid breaches. Developments in the fields of Internet must be taken into account for future requirements. Journalists must be accredited to the DPR for not only greater access but also their accountability. Specialisation in defence reporting is one area where the media has to make concerted efforts to optimise. For it to fructify, training a few dedicated media men will have to be undertaken.

Media Policy

In the words of B G Verghese[1], media without a policy is like a horse without a rider. A policy needs to be formulated taking into account all those factors that need attention now or will require an indulgence in the future. Pragmatic approach to define the parameters and laying down the terms of references will have to be as unambiguous as they can be. Phrases like 'national-security' and 'national-interest' remain a constant source of dilemma in times of rapidly changing environment during war and peace. Anything and everything can fall within the ambit of such a definition and, thus, effectively preventing the spread of information. Arrest of the flow of information through these veiled filters denigrates the environment besides affecting the much desirable credibility of the media.

Bandwidth of the spectrum of media has undergone a vast expansion and the length and breadth of it now contains not only the newspapers, magazines, periodicals in a multitude of languages, radio, television and the internet but also the cellular phones with SMS and internet email capabilities. Innovative ideas backed with vested interests may sometimes lead the horse without a rider to a catastrophe. Safeguards to ensure a frictionless functioning of the machinery without sparks remain a concern for the policy makers. Besides the checks and balances, entire machinery in itself requires to be oiled for its smooth functioning and also to prevent its rusting and jamming.

Media policy will clearly have to spell the do's and don'ts in general and very specially in the matters of defence reporting. War and peace both require an apt handling of a fast developing situation. Engagement of the media to wash the dirt out is perfectly fine but not when it becomes permanently routine in nature. It is rather more applicable when the media is required to switch roles from peace to war reporting; as sustained criticism at all times till the war generates a need to guard national interest may lend it on to an absolutely opposite platform. Policy makers will do well to integrate the guidelines and the enforcement structure taking into account the varying needs of the regional, national and the international media. A balance of the continuum on whose one end are the facts and on the other is the need for psychological warfare (psyops) during trying times, must be obtained through appropriate guidelines in the policy. It will have to be ensured that the media has the first strike capability.[2] Public opinion needs to be aroused in favour of friendly forces and political and economic pressures must be generated against opponent's operation besides influencing opponent's strategy and tactics through information denial, exploitation and dis-information.[3] Adequate safeguards have to be built in the policy to ensure a study of opponent's support of opposition elements against own operations. Efficiency of the adversaries needs to be targeted by encouraging dissatisfaction among potentially dissident elements.[4] Templates are required to be worked out well in advance catering for multiple needs and different situations and, to borrow a military phrase, sand modeling must be done to iron out the imperfections.

Ban on Media

Ban on media must not be imposed as it ill serves the very purpose it is designed to achieve. Should the situation so demand it, the policy regarding the imposition of any ban or restrictions on the movement of media personnel must be clear, unambiguous and non-discriminatory in nature. Transparency about the reasons for any restrictions must always be maintained.

Accreditation

A list of accredited defence journalists must be made and such list should be available at the media camps and centres. Media is as nationalistic in their approach as the military However, there may be a need to remain watchful against those who may indulge in harmful reporting either at the behest of vested interest parties or even unwittingly. Renewal of accreditation must take into account the past record and the reputation of the particular journalist. Like any other profession where a license or a degree is needed before being allowed to practice; the same must be ensured by the media barons for greater accountability and professionalism especially at the beginner's level.

Restructuring the Organisation

Duplication or multiplicity in handling the effective flow of information in itself is self-defeating. There should be only one agency dealing with the requirements. An integrated approach to design the structure interacting with the media must be taken where a central point will be needed to give the desired broad information and to further channel the media to appropriate levels. Different tiers and tentacles will of course be required to formulate, assist and satisfy the information managers besides analysing it for its appropriate content without loosing the speed and its effectiveness.

Notwithstanding the effective functioning of the ALC during Operation Vijay; duality and overlapping of responsibility between the DPR and the ALC not only created a conflictual situation but also rendered one of the two agencies to stick to only arranging the administration for the tour of the journalists to the battlefront.

Daily briefing on the television was definitely an excellent idea but it stopped with the end of the conflict in Kargil. It needs to be continued occasionally, during the normal period too, and as and when the situation so demands.

Proper selection of the Public Relation Officer (PRO) is a very important requirement; he is the first person who is contacted by the people in the media. Generally, through him flows the entire information. Often, the media has voiced their concerns about this fact and have dubbed the PRO as too inexperienced and ineffective a person. A section of the media also feels that the Army does not take its PROs seriously.[5] PROs will have to be senior enough to be able to interact and get the desired information from the right quarters of the Army hierarchy, with speed. He must also be a professional communicator.[6] For this the level of PROs needs to be raised. Mr JN Dixit, Mr G Parthasrthy and Mr S Haider all were PROs of the Ministry of External Affairs.[7] As the entire image of the Army is projected through him, a most stringent selection process must be put in place before an officer is posted as a PRO.[8]

Selection and Grooming of PROs

It is suggested that at a service bracket of eight to ten years volunteer officers must be called up to undertake a written exam followed by an interview. His selection will also have to take into account his past service records wherein his flair and suitability for such a job will have to be seen. An induction of five to six such officers per year would add up to a pool of talent. These officers must undergo a two years journalists' course at a mass communication institute such as the Indian Institute of Mass Communication, at New Delhi. To further hone their skills and understand the functioning of the mass media, these officers must then be allowed to function as assistants to senior defence correspondents in the mainstream of the national media. Such an exposure would not only be the on-job-training but would also form an investment into development of working relationship with the media. Only thereafter these officers should be posted back as regional PROs. To look after their career interests, these officers will have to be guaranteed certain rank before retiring, albeit subject to good performance and without waiting for any command assignments. These officers will ultimately be forming a defence correspondent pool available to the mass media in general who have the requisite experience of both the sides and, thus, fulfilling the existing void in this field. The Qualitative Requirements (QRs) for PROs can be drawn by the Military Secretary's branch in the Army Headquarters.

Training for and of the Media

One of the senior officers of the Indian Army has opined in his latest book that, "*The Kargil conflict has proved beyond doubt that while the media persons lack training in military affairs and war reporting, armed forces lacked training and preparedness to facilitate the task of media and counter information. There is, therefore, a compelling need for them to carry out serious introspection to understand each other's characteristics. Then only will they be able to function as partners in the same enterprise.*"[9]

These observations are true and the fact remains that media as well the military have to train for each other. For a fruitful and integrated interaction with the media, the Army will have to seriously consider training its junior as well as senior officers at each level besides working out a workable programme of training the men in the media. The training in the army will have to begin at the academy level albeit in its basic form. Courses like the Junior Command (JC), Senior Command (SC) and the Higher Command (HC) are the ideal platforms to educate officers about the nuances of interaction with the media. All these courses must have a short capsule or programme of media interaction after each battle related sand model discussion. The practice of allowing only a select rank to interact with the media must be discontinued as it only serves to delay passing the correct information. If at all a filter is required to prevent confidential information becoming public, it must be done at a central level whereby the media will be required to publish/broadcast the news only after it has been vetted.

On the other hand, the media must be given full opportunity to be associated and trained in matters military. On an annual basis, select correspondents who are fresh, could be attached to various units for the duration of two to four weeks. Not only this training will ensure fresh media persons to know the Army and its functioning better but also help in forging a life long bond with the particular unit. As and when the time comes, these very media personnel will be available to be clubbed with the units as 'embedded journalists'.[10] We might recall that during the two World Wars, the war correspondent has traditionally regarded himself as a loyal auxiliary to his nation's armed forces and American correspondents even wore military uniforms. Although reporters are supposed to be noncombatants, from Richard Harding Davis at Las Guasimas to Charles Mohr at Hue, they have carried weapons and joined in assaults.[11] On the battlefield, the Defence Correspondents may be allowed to wear army uniform with the insignia of 'Media'.

Defence Correspondents' Course (DCC) at College of Combat or the Army War College, as it is now known, has been off and on from time to time. It must now be revived in keeping with times. Basic problem faced by the media is sparing the individual for a long duration, that too far away from their bases of operations.[12] The result has been either an under subscription of the vacancies on the course or the new entrants only attending this training capsule, who may or may not necessarily be reporting on defence matters in the near future. What is needed is a fresh approach to the DCC. The course or the capsule must be run at major media centres such as New Delhi, Calcutta, Lucknow, Pune, Mumbai, Bangalore and Chennai. Almost at each of these places the Army has some presence which could be entrusted with a common syllabus and a schedule of training events drawn by the Army Training Command (ARTRAC). These capsules may be run for a week or ten days in each quarter of the year. The timings will have to be either in the forenoons or the afternoons so that the media persons are available to attend to their daily chores besides getting to know the Army better.[13]

Frontline and Target End Presence of Media

Every battle, conflict or war will have width as well as depth.[14] Unusual thing happened at Kargil. The military as well as media will have to factor this into their planning. Unlike the case in Kargil, the distance between the forward troops and the target end will be increasing with the advancement of weaponry. Thus, a need for the media to take appropriate measures to strike a balance between the need to be with the forward troops and at the target end.[15] American war on terrorism in Afghanistan has amply demonstrated the large distance between the forward troops who were as far as the Indian Ocean or even beyond while the targets lay in the interiors of Afghanistan. The war on Iraq has shown the need for the media to be present with the frontline troops as well as at the target end. What it further suggests is the inescapable requirement for the media to be equally techno-savvy and ready for any eventuality.

Background Information

Kargil was an obscure place, least known and, for some, it existed only on the maps without any significance, until the battle when the world took a note of it. To the men in media not much of background information was available. Even maps of the area were not readily available for distribution to those media men who wanted it. In borrowed words, the background information on each of these areas must all be ready for distribution beforehand and thereafter. Even if an Eskimo were to come and report on the situation, he should be able to do so with ease.[16] What it translates to the local military headquarters is the need to prepare such handouts/maps/charts in advance and keep them ready for use in times of need. Firstly, it will give enough information to the media to open their account without loosing time and, secondly, it will result in understanding of the battle with ease not only by the media but by the public as well.

Media Camps and Centres

Unlike the 1971 Operations, there were no media camps or centres during the battle in Kargil. Everyone from the media either converged on to Srinagar, Dras or Kargil. Also, the media had to fend for themselves in hotels in Kargil town. Journalists at times found themselves stranded on the roadside with no help available. This probably was one of the reasons for the journalists not to cross over to Batalik and Turtok areas and the result was that both the areas remained ignored for quite some time during the battle. Unfortunately again, there were no regular and institutionalised briefings once inside the battle zone.

Certainly, there is a case for ensuring establishment of media camps or centres in various sectors. Standard Operating Procedures (SOPs) must be laid down to establish such camps or centres during and even for some time after the war is over. Flow of relevant information from the fighting troops to the camps or centres must be ensured. Timings for regular daily briefings must be laid down as well as an update on any development in the situation to be given out during the briefing. Such a procedure would ensure a regulated flow of information as well as that of the men in media. Institutionalised briefings will also serve to negate the need to further sensor the information.

It would definitely be a good idea to have some temporary shelters available in a secured place in the battlezone for those journalists who are stranded en route for some reasons. Some of the journalists have gone as far as to suggest the need for catering the complete logistics for the media. Also, they feel that the expenditure thus incurred be treated as part of the war effort.

Matters of Command

Discussion in the media about each and every decision and remarks made by a senior commander on the battlefield has to be done with care and caution that it deserves. As the implications are pregnant with a possibility of an undue pressure on the commander, thus, resulting in diverting his attention from applying himself to the problems of day to day battle. It would be wiser to allow him to follow a course of action which he deems appropriate as he is the most competent person to do so and that is why he has been placed there. A free counsel available through the media may temptingly be distractive the least. A just, fair and careful criticism in the media, on the other hand, may exert the right amount of pressure on the decision-makers. What is evident is the right balance in reporting such matters.

Lack of Equipment

War is not the right time to focus on the absence or lack of right equipment. The need is to build in the checks and balances that are applied during peacetime. Regular weekly columns in newspapers, magazines, periodicals and programmes on radio and television must be dedicated to the needs of the armed forces. We do have regular columns and programmes on films, sports and the likes, but not on the armed forces! Any shortfall or weakness would be easier to remove and made up well in time through such programmes. What armed forces need is the right equipment at the right time and the media can play a very vital role in this field.

Media Coverage

Television channels, radio, newspapers, magazine and periodicals devoted major part of their reportage on Kargil battle and related stories. Although television channels proliferated as a result, yet the contribution of another important member of the broadcast media; the Radio, has not adequately been noticed. While the television was omnipresent, the access to the latest in news and the personal messages on the heights such as Tololing, Tiger Hill or Jubar Hill was through the radio or the pocket transistors which soldiers generally carried for listening to news and entertainment programmes. There were instances when the soldiers heard messages from their near and dear ones on the radio. It was not only the Vividh Bharati that entertained them, other radio stations played their role in sustenance of the soldiers morale by keeping them linked to their homes. On those heights one could tune his radio easily to Vijayawada, Chennai or many other such stations from further down south of the country. As a matter of fact, the regular programme 'Forces Request', on radio station Delhi 'B' has been immensely popular in Siachen.[17]

Under such conditions, neither the newspapers or magazines or periodicals nor the television has a reach as compared to the radio that scored way above the rest. Thus, indicating a potential strong tool that could turn the tide in favour or against. It is difficult to conduct a survey of the effect radio had on the fighting qualities and morale of a soldier, yet it may not be out of place to rank it higher than the rest as far as the soldiers on the front and its reach are concerned. Penetration of the radio among the masses is possibly the largest and even larger than all the other media put together. Policy makers have to take a note of this fact when drawing out a media policy. A 24 hours round the clock radio station completely dedicated to the armed forces is an idea that must be taken very seriously; through this the monotony of the normal peace-time field tenure could be minimised. Also, radio would serve as an alternate method to reach soldiers easily on the front. A small pocket transistor as a standard item of the kit of a soldier may prove to be well worth the investments.

Media Pool

Creation of a 'Media Pool' may be considered after a careful study of the system that worked (or did not work as per some researchers) during the Gulf War in 1991. The Media Pool concept was first tried out in combat by the Americans in December 1989, during Operation Just Cause in Panama which was a mixed success for the pool.[18] National Media Pool was set up after the 1983 US military operations in Grenada. While Grenada was a military success, it was a journalistic disaster, because reporters were kept off the island until the fighting was over.[19] The procedure for Gulf War included the reporter sending his dispatch from the war zone after a review by a military Public Affairs Officer,[20] who ensured the operational security and troop's safety. Thereafter Press Centre at Dahran released it. If military public affairs officer believed information in the story violated any ground rules, public affairs officers at Dahran Press Centre reviewed it before release. If they too believed, they appealed to Pentagon bureau chiefs or editors who were then called up to discuss the story. Quick disposal was however ensured.[21] A similar system can be planned; albeit modifications to the system to suit our requirements will have to be worked out in consultation with the media. Also, we have to take into account the media related lessons from the recent War on Iraq.

Behaviour With Locals

War must not create new alienation by commandeering mules, buses, trucks, and houses etc. If casual labour is hired rules must exist to pay them in time. Similarly, for hiring civil transport or residential premises adequate compensation must be planned and paid before it is too late. Media can play a very important role here by highlighting the inadvertent lapses well in time. Although not a case in Kargil, the policing of local area is better left for the Police. The military must avoid getting involved into it as it may result in their getting alienated. When necessary, the support will be required from all quarters including that of the media.

Ground Rules

We need to also evolve certain ground rules for stories from the war zone. Some of the guidelines are as follows:-

(a) Details of future operations must not be disclosed.

(b) Specific information about troop's strength or location must never be made public.

(c) Details of troops movements or tactics while a specific Operation is under way must not be disclosed.[22]

(d) Own operational weaknesses that could be used against own troops by the adversaries must never be discussed until the end of the operations.

(e) Live reporting of events and breaking of news that may lend to losing of the operational surprise must be done only after necessary clearance.

(f) Investigative reporting to find out an apparent missing link in the battle zone must be done with a caution, as it might be by design.

(g) Discussion of the personalities or leadership in the middle of the war better be avoided till the battle is over.

(h) Media rivalries must shift from the battlefield to the football or the cricket fields.

(j) A balanced focus on the entire war zone must be made lest it results into strategic or tactical operational imbalance on ground due to undue attention being paid to a relatively less important sector.

(k) One of the most important factors is the morale of the troops who are fighting the battle; all news stories must be weighed against this factor. Gossips, rumours and loose talks are better avoided until confirmed by the authorised agencies.

An effort had been made to look at the factors that contribute or inhibit the traditional media and military interaction and all that went into making Kargil a success story - both in terms of military operations as well as the role played by the media. Some of the basic assumptions have proved to be either a fallacy or established as facts in this research. At the same time some new facts or ideas have emerged. It is only time that will test the authenticity of some of the remarks or observations. However, by no means the research is comprehensive enough to not allow further additions or even deletions. Newer ideas and methods will still be tried out and the process of evolution will go on.

In the end, one could say that media did emerge as a force-multiplier for the military without succumbing to the official hierarchy. An all out effort must be made for this success to be replicated without loosing sight of the lessons learnt during Kargil as well as those learnt from previous conflicts. We must also keep pace with the fast moving technological changes and take appropriate measures without getting surprised on this count.

References

1. In conversation with the author.
2. Mr BG Verghese in conversation with the author on 1 March 2002.
3. Brig Subhash Chander, "Info-War : Psychological Dimension", *NDC Papers 1/98,* p. 60.
4. *Ibid.*
5. Dinesh Kumar, "Soldiers and Scribblers- Media in Information Warfare: A Case Study of India", *Occasional Paper Series*, IDSA (June 2001), p. 23.
6. n. 2.
7. AG Noorani, "The Defence Services and the Media", *Trishul*, Vol. IV, No. 2 (December 1991), p. 84.
8. *Ibid.*
9. Maj Gen Samay Ram, *Tackling Insurgency and Terrorism* (New Delhi: Manas, 2002), p.103.
10. Coalition Forces in the latest War on Iraq have used this concept albeit with their own modifications and as per Herald-Argus website 500 reporters were embedded with military units during the war.
11. Arthur Lubow, "Read Some About It", in Hedrick Smith (ed), *The Media and the Gulf War : The Press and Democracy in Wartime* (Washington DC: Seven Locks Press, 1992), p. 98.
12. Kieth Flory, Senior Editor *The Pioneer* in conversation with the author.
13. *Ibid.*
14. n. 2.
15. R Prasannan, Editor, *The Week,* in conversation with the author.
16. n. 2.

17. Author's own battalion, 27 RAJPUT, regularly listened to 'Forces' Request' when deployed in Siachen during Operation VIJAY.

18. Pete Williams, "Statement Before the US Senate Committee on Governmental Affairs", in Hedrick Smith (ed), n. 11, p. 35.

19. *Ibid*, p. 34.

20. Public Affairs Officers are trained at Fort Benjamin Harrison, and all major commands have graduates of School to act as a bridge between the warrior and the scribe. Installations and War Colleges sponsor symposia and workshops to improve relations with the media. Special tours of military installations and activities are conducted for the Press by the Defence Department and Services and some components of Fourth Estate even reciprocate. Lt Gen Bernard E Trainor (Retd), US Marine Corps, *"The Military and Media A Troubled Embrace"*, in Hedrick Smith (ed), n.11, p. 75.

21. Information has been compiled from the book by Hedrick Smith (ed), n.11.

22. Hedrick Smith (ed), n.11.

Appendix A

Kargil Review Committee Report – From Surprise to Reckoning – Extracts

Media Relations

11.4 How then did India fare with regard to information policy and media relations in Kargil? Perhaps fairly well in some respects, but not well enough. The full dimensions of the Kargil episode and its implications were not gauged or properly appreciated by the media for weeks after the first discovery of the intruders until the Indian Air Force was committed on May 26. Till then, Kargil was perceived as more of the same as before – infiltration. This was pretty well the political and military understanding too until maybe the previous week. The downing of an Indian helicopter and two MIGs by shoulder-fired Stinger missiles shattered this illusion. This was war.

11.5 The metropolitan papers and electronic channels sought to rush their mainline correspondents to the scene of action and the first frontline stories appeared early in June. Passes issued by the Defence Ministry in Delhi were not always honoured, or not too promptly, in Srinagar and beyond. Those who by-passed Zojila to fly to Leh and thence take a taxi to Batalik, Kargil and Dras did better. Facilities and briefing arrangements were limited and correspondents tell of picking up stray bits of information or reactions from junior officers and locals. Uniquely, the Srinagar-Leh National Highway IA was the front. It was the main axis of lateral military movement and supply, the location of the Brigade and Division Headquarters, gun emplacements spewing fire at the enemy, the District headquarters and other townships, the bazaar, the place to access

Source: Kargil Review Committee Report – From Surprise to Reckoning (Government of India, 15 December 1999).

the rare fax and phone facility, and Kargil's one and only Hotel Siachen. Everything happened on the Highway when it was not being bombarded, which it was intermittently, resulting in casualties, civil damage and evacuee movement.

11.6 In some ways, the "war" story wrote itself and it was no surprise that some less experienced reporters were taken in by gossip which was sometimes, but not always, edited out at the other end. There was no media cell to assist reporters. And few of the correspondents at the front had the benefit of training in war reporting.

11.7 There was some briefing for the J&K press in Srinagar and Jammu but the local press felt discriminated against and left out. The local correspondents of the national press were also aggrieved by the fact that preference was given to facilitating coverage by their headquarter colleagues who might fly in from Delhi, be provided assistance to cover one sector or other of the Kargil heights, and then fly out. There was also dismay over TV channels with an international reach being given special facilities, obviously in order to ensure wider coverage which served a national purpose, a consideration that the local reporter understandably did not take to very kindly.

11.8 What this therefore suggests is the need for ensuring suitable facilities for all levels of coverage – local, national and international, the last both from India as well as abroad.

11.9 In Delhi, the routine briefing conducted by the Ministry of Defence was upgraded at the end of May and, instead, jointly taken by senior Army and Air Force spokesmen together with the Foreign Office spokesman on a daily basis. This certainly was an improvement. However, more regular and wider high level background briefings to editors, senior reporters and military commentators should be planned in future for a war situation, and these briefings should be held, from time to time, even in the proxy war situation. Press kits with appropriate background – e.g., of the Kashmir dispute, the LOC, the terrain, maps, texts of Lahore and Simla Agreements, etc – should have been available for distribution and would have been widely cited and filed for future reference. A lot of reporters went into the story blind a reflection as much on their own prepararion and access to essential background as on the kind of backup the official information services provided.

11.10 Some of the Kargil coverage in the aftermath of the Pakistan withdrawal was unfortunately affected by the pre-election politicisation of the issue

The former Commander 121 Brigade, who was in the eye of a media storm, informed the Committee that he was seriously embarrassed by some of what was attributed to him, including letters which he claims he never wrote.

11.11 The grievances of the Jammu and Srinagar media need to be viewed with sympathy. The local media is functioning under the constraint of threats of violence that have not abated. It should not be disregarded or discriminated against in terms of access and facilities as it is the principal means of reaching the people of Jammu and Kashmir. The electronic media has perhaps an even more critical role in the State in view of difficulties of communication. AIR's Kargil transmitter was hit by a shell but recommissioned. The local Station Director felt it would be useful to provide it with a small underground studio as it could be in the line of fire whenever Kargil is bombarded from across the LOC.

11.12 The Union Government has decided to invest over Rs. 400 crores to expand and strengthen AIR and Doordarshan's facilities in the border areas of J&K so as to reach out to people in remote and isolated hamlets and to the population on the other side. While this is welcome, as some Pakistan radio stations like Skardu are clearly heard on the Indian side, the Committee was informed that Prasar Bharati in J&K lacks Balti and other linguistic skills to reach people across the LOC. Unless such software and programming aspects are taken care of, mere hardware expansion may not be cost effective.

11.13 Altogether, both sides of the information equation need to be strengthened in J&K and other areas of militant violence and insurgency. Transparency and improved information flows can help promote morale, understanding and reconciliation. Security and Defence related public relations must be improved at all levels and the media provided suitable training facilities in order to enable it to do a better job of military coverage. Prompt and timely information is necessary when news is increasingly transmitted and used instantly, with news on the hour, every hour. Delay invariably means having to react to the opponent who is able to portray and interpret the news in the most favourable light from his point of view. This is what happened with the downing of the Pakistan maritime spy plane, the Atlantic, which had intruded into Indian air space in Kutch in August.

11.14 Credibility is as important as access and speed. The contrast in coverage of Operations BLUE STAR and BLACK THUNDER in Amritsar at the height of the Punjab crisis and the impact these made on the public mind is striking.

11.15 Although Kashmir looms so large as a national issue, public relations in this regard remain poor in the matter of a range of details. The two Ministers who spoke for India on Kashmir in the BBC's programme, Hard Talk, were inadequately briefed for their grilling on human rights in and idea of mediation on Kashmir in the midst of the Kargil confrontation when international sympathy was by and large with India and Pakistan stood isolated. Satyameva Jayate is an excellent motto. But the truth must be assisted to prevail.

11.16 The ban on cable operators showing Pakistan TV and on VSNL providing access to the Karachi paper *Dawn's* website on Internet appeared to be a knee-jerk reaction and not particularly well considered. Pakistan was able to portray these as acts of Indian censorship for fear of the "truth" whereas PTV's falsification of news from Kargil would have been the best antidote to its crude propaganda.

VI. Media Relations and Information

13.73 If the media served the country well, much of the credit goes to the initiative it itself took and to some individuals within the Government and the Armed Forces. Information is power, especially in this Information Age. The media moulds national and international opinion and can be a potent force multiplier. This was evident at Kargil – India's first television war. All things considered coverage by the print and electronic media was by and large satisfactory. Yet it was apparent that, with some exceptions, media personnel lacked training in military affairs and war reporting and that the Armed Services lacked training and preparedness to facilitate the task of the media and counter misinformation.

13.74 Defence Public Relations are routinely handled by the Ministry of Defence through regular Information service cadres. This establishment is not equipped to handle media relations during war or even proxy war. The briefing function during the Kargil crisis was taken over by a triad of senior military and civil spokesmen. Army Headquarters set up an Information and Psychological Warfare Cell under an officer of the rank of Major General with direct access to the Army Chief. This enabled Army Headquarters both to monitor and disseminate information in a better-calibrated manner than would have been the case otherwise.

13.75 Reporting on the campaign revealed a lack of public information about the command structure of the Armed Forces and how responsibilities are distributed within the national intelligence framework. While arrangements were made for official briefings at Delhi, there were inadequate arrangements at the Corps, Division and Brigade levels. Nor were there arrangements to brief officers and men at the ground level on daily developments nor to interface with the civil authorities. The result was generation of a lot of inaccurate information such as the reported capture of a number of Indian Army bunkers (whereas the enemy only occupied one permanent patrol post which had earlier been vacated on account of extreme weather conditions), the existence of three-storyed enemy bunkers equipped with television sets, and the purchase by the intruders of cement from the Dras-Kargil market.

13.76 A number of simple misperceptions became apparent in newspaper reports questioning the absence of the Army Chief in Poland during the early part of May 1999 and the Northern Army Commander going to Pune about the same time. The early military appreciation was of limited infiltration in Kargil. Nevertheless, the Corps Commander, in whose area of responsibility the intrusion (as it was subsequently discovered to be) occurred, had acted promptly and vigorously to deal with even larger eventualities. There was no need to cancel the Army Chief's visit, which had been long planned and was of some political significance. The COAS remained in touch with developments at home and there was no vacuum in the higher military leadership because of his absence abroad during the early phase of Kargil developments. The Army Commander, in turn, went to Pune for a briefing from his predecessor, Lieutenant General S. Padmanabhan, now Southern Army Commander. He too was in constant touch with his Command and HQ 15 Corps and had already set in motion various precautionary measures.

13.77 Some of all this is inevitable in the fog of war. But efforts have to be made to review information handling procedures within the Armed Forces and their public dissemination. The Army needs such improved public relations capability even otherwise when deployed on counter-insurgency duties. Public relations are presently managed by the Ministry of Defence and at the formation level by military officers who have no media background.

13.78 A comprehensive account of the Kargil operations remains to be brought out. Pakistani political and military leaders have repeatedly highlighted their nuclear capability and their will to use it. Accounts have also appeared in Pakistan of how India was thrice deterred by its nuclear capability. India's reticence in setting the record straight about the earlier conflicts and the developments in the nuclear field appear to have influenced the Pakistani mindset and led to the adventurous miscalculation over Kargil.

13.79 The first overall briefing on the Kargil situation in the Military Operations Room was given to the Defence and External Affairs Ministers on May 17 with the Chiefs of Staff Committee in attendance. This was followed by a meeting of the Cabinet Committee on Security (CCS) chaired by the Prime Minister on May 18 and a briefing of the Prime Minister and Defence Minister on May 24, with the COSC in attendance, by when the magnitude of the Kargil intrusion had been more or less fully assessed. The Army Chief had returned from Poland by May 20 when the CCs met again on May 25*, with the

* CCS met formally only on May 25, 1999; earlier meetings of May 1999 were briefing sessions.

COSC in attendance, and the use of the air power was cleared.

13.80 War and proxy war does not leave the civil population untouched. Human rights violations, civilian casualties, destruction or commandeering of property, refugee movements and the disruption of infrastructure and livelihoods must be expected. This calls for the creation of a civil-military interface at various levels to deal with a whole range of problems on an emergency basis. Such liaison was lacking during the Kargil action and points to a deficiency that must be made good.

13.81 The outcome of the Kargil operation was both a military and diplomatic triumph for India. The Pakistani intruders were evicted with heavier casualties than those suffered by India. The sanctity of the LOC received international recognition and Pakistan was isolated in the comity of nations. While attending to such shortcomings as have been brought to light, the nation can be proud of the manner in which the Armed Forces and the people as a whole acquitted themselves.

Appendix B

Reforming The National Security System – Extracts

Media Relations

6.83 The MoD must have an organisation integral to it for interface with the media on defence related issues. It should therefore evolve the precise details of the structure, composition and modalities of functioning of this entity. For this purpose it may draw appropriate personnel from other organisations, if considered necessary. Media cells should also be set up by the MoD in states or at places where they are required, such as in the field formations, up to an appropriate level.

6.84 The MoD should have standing instructions or provisions in the relevant manual specifying to what extent and in what situations the Armed Forces should take the initiative to invite media teams to cover activities of the Armed Forces in conflict situations and in such cases, what information/material should be made available to them (including what material/information should not be shared with them) and what facilities should be extended to them. The media in the country has been consistently favourably inclined to the Armed Forces and a more forth coming approach is not only justified but essential, to ensure better informed reporting and positive coverage.

6.85 As and when media teams are invited by the Armed Forces (all three wings) in peace and conflict situations to places where operations are being conducted, the latter should provide local transport and boarding/lodging facilities, as in border or conflict areas where civilian infrastructure or facilities are not available.

Source:Reforming The National Security System – Recommendations of Group of Ministers (February 2001).

Appendix C

Media and National Security – Extracts

Mr Shekhar Gupta, Editor-in-Chief, The Indian Express

"Another major area of research is the new battlefield. What is the new battlefield? How does it differ from the old battlefield? It is not precision guided or stand off weapons. These are all old issues. The new battlefield is the battlefield under the constant glare of the media. It is now presumed that in future no commander will be able to conduct any combat without the live attention of the media."

"The Iraq Gulf War, also termed the Second Gulf War was one where the media was kept at bay by General Norman Schwerzpkof, but they still ate out of his hands, is the kind of an ideal situation that any battlefield commander of tomorrow would want during war. I was present during that war and the myth is that actually there was no war during the Second Gulf war... There was no real war. If a real war had taken place resulting in the loss of a couple of hundred American lives and ten to twenty tanks, media management would have collapsed. He would have had no time to handle the media and media would have discovered adequate confusion to get stories of their own."

"It is often stated that two democracies never go to war with each other. In Kargil we went to war with Pakistan, but Pakistan, ideally cannot be termed as a democracy. In the words of a very articulate Pakistani politician who would rather not have the description attributed to him, Pakistan can at best be termed as a 'Bonsai Democracy'."

Source : Minutes of ARTRAC Seminar on Media and National Security held at IIMC, New Delhi 27-28 September 2000.

"In 1988 Mr KPS Gill, tha same gentleman who had been worried about two journalists on the banks of a river put two hundred journalists on the terrace of Guru Nanak Niwas to watch Operation Black Thunder. He gave us binoculars for a clearer view and permitted us free access to the NSG Control Room. He had learnt a lesson through the Blue Star. In comparison Black Thunder is a lesson we must all learn."

"Today, because our media is seen to be free, **during Kargil, BBC and CNN simply didn't make that kind of impact. We almost never turned to the BBC and CNN for news on Kargil and instead watched Star and Zee TV. The surprising thing and the most telling one is that so did the Pakistanis. During the war the average Pakistani believed Star or Zee TV more than PTV and also never felt the need to view BBC or CNN** (emphasis added) for information because he felt that if the Indian cameras showed all what was going wrong in India and other criticalities were also being voiced, obviously it was telling the truth."

"My humble submission is that no matter what happens, regardless of laws and restrictions it will not be possible to conduct any war, external or internal without the presence of media, seeing the way the technology is progressing…The battlefield of the future can not be hidden from the media under any circumstances. **The media, like diabetes, is a part of our lives. You can not cure the disease but you can learn to live with it** (emphasis added). If you learn to live with the media in a positive manner it will work well both ways."

"If your media has access to information and is trusted by your countrymen and internationally, people will stop believing rumours and will not wait for Mark Tully or the BBC to tell them what they perceive as the truth. Please do survey the Kargil period and the popular perception post Kargil. Look at the manner in which the BBC and CNN ratings have fallen. **Kargil has done for the Indian electronic media what the Gulf War had done for the CNN** (emphasis added). The heads of both, the BBC and CNN have visited India thrice during last one year complaining that no one seemed to be watching their news."

"Finally, while I urge upon you to do all the above, learn to communicate with us and share information with us. There are a few things you must not do:-

- Never share with the media any operational plans. Just tell us the truth about the events. The media is not trained to share secrets and journalists being brags by nature may tend to reveal secrets in unguarded moments.
- **Please do not treat the media as a force multiplier** (emphasis added). The media is not a part of the Armed Forces and this will lead to a loss of credibility. The problem during Kargil was that, during the final stages of conflict the media coverage became akin to propaganda, not for any fault of the Army, but, the media persons living with the Army happened to speak like the Army PROs. This indeed was unfortunate and some of them had to be restrained. ...So, while the media did play a role of a force multiplier (emphasis added),... it is not our role. It is a role, which is presumed that we will play."

"Kargil has thrown up some questions. As long as there are twenty to thirty casualties a day, it is fine (sic) but God forbid, if in a war there are five hundred casualties a day, the whole situation will need a re-look. **The media can be a force multiplier or a shock absorber** (emphasis added). We can be both of these if you deal with us as with any other institution of the Government or any section of the society, in the correct manner, following the principles of our profession as you follow yours."

"Kargil has shown a very serious shortcoming. Even in a localised war we found a shortage of trained persons to cover the same. The media will find it extremely difficult to cover a large scale conflict...If there is anything the media can do, I assure you of our cooperation on behalf of all media institutions, Indian Newspaper Society, Editors' Guild etc. **You show the way but never presume that we are a force multiplier and never use the term media management** (emphasis added). It is self-defeating as culturally and genetically, the media is unmanageable. The free media can never be managed."

"If work on the principle of mutual intersection it will be very good for us and also for national interests. May I wish you all the very best and promise you that the **media is willing to go an extra mile in its own simple way** (emphasis added)."

Mr K Subrahmanyam

"The Kargil Committee Review Panel submitted a report of seventeen volumes with appendices to the Government. It was submitted for immediate release to the public. The appendices have not been released and even in the report there have been deletions, some of them being laughable ones. For example, the names of the two shepherds who were supposed to have reported the intrusions have been deleted on the grounds that sources are not mentioned. The names of twenty individuals have been mentioned in twenty books and those books state that the Army had no knowledge of the intrusions and that these were discovered by two shepherds. The two shepherds were detained by the Brigade Intelligence Team. Mentioning this would have been to the credit of the Army and the Government."

"The Kargil Report was placed in the Parliament on 25 Feb 2000 for discussion. The Indian Nuclear Doctrine was released on 19 Aug 99 to be discussed in the Parliament. You will realize that it is not merely a question of the relationship of media and the Armed Forces. It is a much bigger issue."

"Today, most media youngsters have strong political alignments...Most of the people have very strong political views, alignments and these influence their reporting. Even today, after the Kargil Conflict you can see the kind of things being written in the newspapers which are not objective."

"Another problem is that the newspapers in this country do not have dedicated defence correspondents. Even those who say they have them cover a large canvas of reporting, home, external affairs and defence. Most of them do not know how the Armed Forces are structured and function. As a result you have some of them saying 'Where was the war? It was a brigade action. Very few people were killed.' But as Mr Chari just said, the Stockholm Peace Research Institute has stated that it just qualifies to be a major arms conflict as the casualties exceeded one thousand. But people said that the Army Chief should have been right at the front and he should have taken some action. This was a war which should have been run by the Corps Commander, the Army Chief looks after national policy. There is a total ignorance of certain defence aspects in the media and some people use it to suit their political alignments. This is a major problem and needs to be addressed."

"People must understand that war reporting in intense and mobile warfare is not feasible. If some one had a UAV it would have been shot down in no time. It is possible only in the kind of war fought in Kargil. People must be clear about what can be covered in a war in a conflict like Kargil or in a proxy war where more can be covered. Then also, it can only be done under an escort provided by the Armed Forces. Now, if that is done there is another problem, you are accused of favouring one side. I have read the Srinagar Press complain that NDTV, Zee TV and the BBC were favoured and the local Press was not. The other reporters were even taken right up to the front and provided with helicopters while the local reporters were not. When told that the Army had inadequate resources and worldwide coverage was to be given making best use of the resources and hence they had to be given preference, the Government only invited adverse comments. How do you deal with such problems when limited resources have to be optimised by the Army. People complained of not having been provided adequate security. Foreign journalists could fly to Leh, take a taxi and cover events while local journalists could not. So, in looking at Kargil as an example where TV coverage took place one must be careful while generalising on Kargil. It was a very unique operation and will not necessarily happen again."

Answering a question from Cdr KS Dalal, USI on strategic partnership with the media, Mr Subrahmanyam said,

"If you are talking of a partnership, personally I would not have used the term. If the media is there it has a role, so, how do we get together to our mutual advantage. You may call it a partnership or you may not do so. Mr Shekhar Gupta also warned us to desist from the term **media management and force multiplier** (emphasis added). The answer is that since the media is reporting you must ensure that it will help you and not harm you. To that extent you must make use of media and that is the way to approach it. **The old idea that media is one of the four major institutions of the nation state is no longer as fashionable as it used to be** (emphasis added)."

Former Military Correspondent of the *Indian Express,* Dr Chengappa, IDSA also added his comments on the above question, when he said, "...media is commercially driven but it is not necessarily a product, it is also a service. So, we must view the media as a service in the Army's relationship with the media."

Lt Gen Satish Nambiar, PVSM, AVSM, VrC (Retd)

"There is recognition that today national security encompasses much more than mere territorial integrity and preventing external military aggression. However, the apparatus remains the same as it was at independence. Integration of the Defence Forces within themselves and with the other agencies that are concerned with national securities can not be **delayed any longer** (emphasis added). The sooner we get to grips with this the better. And in this endeavour, both the Armed Forces and the media have **complimentary roles to play** (emphasis added)."

While replying to a question on the Army's attitude in lack of transparency towards the media, Lt Gen Nambiar said, "If instructions are issued by the Ministry of Defence laying down guidelines for interaction with the media, the issue will be resolved and all anomalies will be removed. **The media policy should be issued** (emphasis added). As long as that is not done any number of media courses for men in uniform will not serve the purpose."

Mr PR Chari

"...there is not only a lack of transparency but also a lack of appreciation of a lack of transparency. How transparency can be used as a force multiplier has been aptly brought out by Mr Shekhar Gupta."

"In Kashmir the external and internal roles are merging and external aggression has been manifested by subversive training, equipment and providing safe sanctuaries to militants."

"The involvement of the Armed Forces in low intensity conflicts requires optimisation of all available instruments and there is an important role for the Armed Forces in administrative and developmental functions to generate local sympathy and which was the philosophy of the Army Development Group. Media needs to be approached through this perspective. I would not suggest that it is **media management** (emphasis added). It is an understanding of what the media is, an approach to the media is possible and they could be used for whatever be your pursuits. Media always needs to disseminate its views objectively. This is a message for the media. But while one hopes that the media disseminates its views objectively, Armed Forces must also appreciate the difficulties of the functioning of the media under normal circumstances."

Mr SK Singh

"Media and National Security and Media – Armed Forces relationship in today's world is a new thing. Napoleon's marshals did not have to think of all this, nor did Marshal Foch during the First World War. But with TV having been globalised and with CNN and BBC World News being called additional permanent members of the Security Council the picture is fairly clear."

" The Internet, the computer, global media and the TV which bring, both war and peace into your drawing room are all extremely capable of building up and running events i.e. management of men, stores, weapons, technology for producing energy, power and nuclear weapons, technology of space, producing satellites and other surveillance assets."

"Today, the world demands globalisation and liberalisation. Better economy demands that the Armed Forces are professionally competent and are capable at the officer level to train men to understand the mission. How does it connect to the media? It connects because reputation depend on the media…If Hitler had won World War II he still wouldn't have been called a major thinker. He was not much of a major thinker. I don't think he was much of a thinker – he was a destructive thinker. I will quote something from Hitler which should impress some of us. He said, 'Mental confusion, contradiction of feelings, indecisiveness, panic which we create in other society – these are our weapons.' We must all have seen the latest edition of the *Outlook* magazine and realised as to what some officers must have briefed them and the great satisfaction it is creating to our West and our North."

"I have been the longest serving spokesman of this country's external affairs from 1969 to 1974 and I like to think that during the Bangla Desh war all the mistakes that were made or might have been made were contained for the sake of national morale, reputation of our Armed forces, reputation of those who had sacrificed their lives or were prepared to sacrifice their lives. Today it is not so...Movark said and I quote, '*The Press engages in diplomacy and diplomacy exerts influence through the Press. The people exposed to this double impact unconsciously guide in various directions or else if it lives to think for itself that society it is bound to fall into errors. The responsibility of the Press is so great that wars if not made by the Government, can be made by the Press.*' I would add made or marred."

Mr KK Katyal

"So far as defence and what is connected with the conduct of war are concerned the media has to build the requisite kind of information and the expertise. We do have some eminent commentators and defence analysts at the senior level. Some good examples can be found in the coverage of the recent conflict but as far as specialisation as war correspondents is concerned or defence as it is known in the Western world, this is yet to be achieved. This is an area which requires deep and sustained effort so that those are required to cover operations are competent and well equipped for the job. As the recent coverage of (Kargil) war indicates the media did rise to the occasion. It also revealed considerable **potential and promise**" (emphasis added).

"The relationship between the media and the Armed Forces is very peculiar...Different norms have to apply to different stages. During times of armed conflict there is some recognition of the media's role but, due to the distance between the Armed Forces and the media during peace time it is not easy to establish a correct equation and that creates problems when the official version is sought to be given of the actual operations. The media finds it too little and too late."

"In the pre and post conflict situations where considerations of the type that obtain during operations do not obtain, the media can afford to be forthright and totally ruthless to bring to light cases of lapses that have been discovered. To do so would not be contrary to national interests."

AVM Kapil Kak, AVSM, VSM (Retd)

"I will also state that if you look globally, the most crucial factor is that media, whether print or electronic, it is not a homogeneous institution.

The globalisation has impacted nothing more than the media revolution. You have Rupert Murdoch who owns not only most of the important newspapers in the US, Britain and Australia but also owns Sky TV. He also owns Twentieth Century Fox and you know what that means globally. You are looking at a paradigm of deep editorialised communication empires which are beyond any regulation. So you see the power of the media and therefore can you use that media as a force multiplier as we in the Armed Forces are very **prone to say** (emphasis added)? In India alone, there are numerous operators right from the national level downwards in different regions, different languages, belonging to various castes, communities, ethnic groups, all with a very different agenda depending on the institution or depending on the ownership."

"It will be right to say that the term **media management is not applicable any more** (emphasis added). The media is highly individualistic, extremely egoistic, opinionated and I will look upon it as a paradigm in which you are able to establish relationship of mutuality."

"When we look at the politico military balance, the security challenges are equally daunting. Kargil is just a year behind us and I don't think you would have post mortemed it adequately but it was undoubtedly **India's first information war** (emphasis added). I personally believe that in Kargil, **the media was to us what CNN was to US during Gulf War** (emphasis added). It opened American eyes to what the media can do to open the public eye to management of national security. It has, in our context enhanced public awareness to national security and demonstrated the positive application of **media power in war time** (emphasis added)."

"One little picture of Squadron Leader Ahuja's three year old son saluting his father's dead body appeared in Los Angeles Times and I was told (by foreign friends) that it did far more than any other media projection would have done. There was a similar picture, I am told, in East Coast newspaper of Mrs Kalia saluting her husband's dead body with tremendous stoic demeanour which was commented upon by half a dozen newspaper barons at that time. This is to say what a picture can do to project the relationship between the media and the Armed Forces in a wartime situation."

"I believe another area where media can contribute is enhancing for the public at large the virtual starving of the Armed Forces of funds from 1987-88 till 1998-99…It required Gen Pervez Musharraf to sensitise the public and the Government to release twenty eight percent extra for the defence budget to obviate a decade long starvation."

"I also believe questions are asked as to why there is not greater transparency, why the threats and challenges are not known to the media. With this audience I must state that the Ministry of Defence publishes an annual report which identifies the threats and challenges to the state. There are numerous papers of the Estimates Committee and the Consultative Committee which cover in great detail the problems of security and for the media to complain of inadequate transparency will not be correct."

"Undoubtedly, the Armed Forces have a halo around them as it should be. They enjoy tremendous admiration of the people. At the same time we must understand that the Armed Forces are extremely image conscious and sensitive to media criticism. Also, the Armed Forces feel that they have been misrepresented and that things are blown out of proportion by the media. These are the Army's views. But I would suggest that the Armed Forces have not yet gained the requisite experience level in management of media."

Ms Aditi Phadnis

"Then came Kargil. Kargil tore us apart for three reasons. As a reporter, I had to judge with insufficient knowledge, whether we had done right or wrong in Kargil, whether we needed to know who was responsible. Why did the war happen? I had to report for negligence and how did the war happen? I had to report the Army in way that was both accurate, patriotic and at times there is a contradiction between the two. How did we do that? We tried to be as accurate as possible. We stuck to the oldest tenets of journalism – when in doubt don't. We tried to be as contemporary as possible. We were under a lot of pressure as a lot of people wanted to know the truth behind Kargil. That means they were not getting the truth. Who was responsible for this? Was there a problem in information dissemination? Was there a problem in understanding the war or was it mis-reporting?"

"You can write, bring people to their knees because of what you write so you have power. This is not palatable to the forces. But by ignoring this fact it is not going to go away, so you have to understand, demystify that power, see how the system works, understand the challenges of the future and understand how it can be a **force multiplier** (emphasis added), a term I have learnt anew and am proud of using."

"The most unfortunate part is that the Army, Navy and the Air Force **do not understand news** (emphasis added). This is my experience. They don't understand news, they don't know how to handle it. They don't know how to use it, anticipate it, they don't know what to do if the news goes against them."

"...if you don't give some thought to information flowing out of the firewall, very quickly it will not be good for either of the two of us (Armed Forces and media)."

Maj Maroof Raza (Retd)

"The 1990's will be remembered as the 'decade of the dish' (after that ubiquitous concave satellite dish, that uplinks major events and gives the viewers a grand stand view of the latest happenings world wide). And it is this peculiar Twentieth Century Military-Media combination of the means of mass destruction and the means of mass communication that has brought the horrors of the battlefield to our living rooms. It also forces the hand of the policy makers, getting them to respond, under the pressure of the TV. But, Governments that pride themselves at their ability to control events and their steadiness of course will be reluctant to admit, that the electronic interloper, TV, plays any part in their decision making."

"There was a time when soldiers would regard the media as a shady lot, in-disciplined, unkempt and unpatriotic and view them with a combination of suspicion and astonishment. Journalism was then regarded as a cover for espionage! But this view is now held by only the orthodox few. Since, most good journalists at the national level see their job as part of their moral commitment to society and with the odd exception, are upright people. And while they, unlike the Army, do not have a written code of ethics, they see their role as follows:-

(a) To create public opinion.

(b) Act as a watch-dog for citizens, specially on human rights issues.

(c) Keep the public informed, with balanced coverage of events.

(d) Maintain national morale by giving responsible news reports."

"Soldiers and journalists are not the most like-minded people, though they are not such different people either. Their relationship though can often be unusual and complex. The media craves for the unusual, since bad news is good news and so, wars will always make headline news. There is however, a need for the Military and the media to understand each other, more importantly, to develop a respect for each other. While the Military on the one hand is insulated and secretive; the media is proud to be open and can **hardly ever keep a secret** (emphasis added)."

"Across the world now, Military institutions have now embarked on a new relationship with the media, since the media moulds national and international opinion, and is a potent **force multiplier** (emphasis added). In this century, they will need each other more than ever before. And this doesn't apply only to the electronic media alone, it also applies to the print and the vernacular media. In fact, it is said that in the Twenty First Century, the most important Military assignments are likely to go to those with an eye for public relations and Military intelligence, and not to those from the combat arms, as has been the case until now. And though there are distant rumblings in case of civil wars, where brinkmanship often precedes the fighting, but wars could come without a warning as it happened in the **Kargil** (emphasis added) conflict between India and Pakistan and journalists will be tempted to rush blindly into a war zone, to get there first for a good story, and not necessarily an accurate report."

"The Gulf War, when satellite TV brought the conflict in 'real-time' to it's viewers and more recently in the Indian context, the Kargil Conflict, India's first TV war, have highlighted that journalists reporting on a conflict cannot make up for their **ignorance with enthusiasm alone** (emphasis added). They do require considerable understanding of the mysterious ways of the Military, and therefore, the need for the media to be better informed about Military affairs. Equally, the Armed Forces must now be trained and prepared to facilitate the tasks of the media, and also to counter dis-information. And the Military would do well to note that **'information is power' in this age of information** (emphasis added)."

"During the Kargil Conflict, the inability of India's Ministry of Defence Public Relations outfit to handle the media, led the Indian Army Headquarters to set up an Information and Public Relations Cell. This enabled the Indian Army to monitor and disseminate information in a calibrated manner, through the conflict. And in a recent debate on the subject of 'Military-Media Relations' at the United Services Institute in New Delhi, some of the issues that emerged in the discussions between a few media men and a larger group of service officers, are as follows:-

(a) National 'interest is not necessarily a monopoly of the establishment, and national security and the interests of the establishment are not always the same thing.

(b) The media often operates at two levels in conflict situations:-

  (i) With a field team that is often respectful towards officers and commanders. .

  (ii) Capital News Agencies that can be quite critical and often dismissive towards the Government.

(c) And while the target audiences for the media in a war could be the international community, to justify the war; in counter Insurgency operations, it is the local population.

(d) Therefore, Military commanders should not only concentrate on just operational issues, but also on public and media relations. In short, information, must be made a Principle of War."

"War reporting is not only a chronicling process, but also a learning process, and as knowledge illuminates new areas of ignorance, the more you know, the more you realise that you do not know. It is, therefore essential in a war, or even in a proxy war situation, for Military Headquarters at all levels to be equipped with 'press kits' and appropriate backgrounders for journalists with maps, information on terrain, enemy deployment and the broad aspects of their strategy which can be revealed without compromising surprise or security, since journalists are not good at keeping secrets."

"So, while denying the media information or waiting too long to structure a correct response, might seem a safe thing from the establishment's point to do, but experience has shown that Governments spend more time making up for the damage caused due to bad press later on. The Military and the establishment must understand that speed is of essence to the electronic media. Since its source of sustenance is its audience, it has to operate by the rules of the market in this 'Consumer Era'. Therefore, if it doesn't get the news it is looking for, media agencies will go to anyone to get their news reports, and can end up even glorifying a terrorist, as they did in the case of **Mast Gul** (emphasis added), the man responsible for burning down the Charar-e-Sharif shrine in 1995, in Kashmir."

"Therefore, what is needed is Military-Media co-operation, and not necessarily a '**management' of the media** (emphasis added). Government agencies and the Armed Forces must accept that :-

(a) There is no such thing as **niche information** (emphasis added), and restricting information to a handful of people serves little purpose; instead, Army formations must broaden their hierarchy for dissemination. Keeping secrets is not so easy anymore; as even friendly agencies do often leak out information since what might be a sensitive issue for the Army in a counter- insurgency operation, might not be so for the police.

(b) Today's modern communication is instant and reliable and bad news to senior commanders could come faster through television or the radio and not from intelligence agencies. It takes just a phone call to reach a newsroom anywhere in the world."

"There are however certain impediments in Military-Media relations. First, the Government/Military establishment has yet to fully appreciate the power of information and the role of media in policy making. And next, the media does not respect social borders and taboos of the past. It is inspired by its own goals, and will go to any lengths to get news to the people, the consumers of information, who deeply **resent any Government control over the media** (emphasis added). Therefore, the media must not be controlled. Holding back information and the banning of media from sensitive areas only leads to bizarre reporting, as the media must report something! The establishment has yet to recognise the importance that terrorists place on news."

"The media they say is "the terrorist's best friend... and as terrorism is aimed at those watching television - as TV declares who is important - terrorists feel that the road to identity is to do something violent..." Therefore, in insurgencies, by using the media selectively, terrorists are able to not only instill fear and insecurity amongst the people, but also create doubts in the minds of the Security Forces about the efficacy of their counter insurgency operations, in turn, making the people and the Military lose faith in the Government. It must be guarded against."

"And so, winning the media over is half the battle, and a 'bonding' with the press is very important. For this the Military must follow **two simple rules** (emphasis added). First, it must respond or confirm a report if it is correct and deny it if it is wrong. It also helps to spell out the follow up action that is at hand such as an operation currently underway or disciplinary action being taken against soldiers in case of misdeeds. Second, soldiers must stick to the facts, however unpleasant they may be and leave analysis to the media. This will only increase their credibility."

"Also, helping the uninformed reporters in the correct identification of military equipment is necessary, as incorrect references by reporters to equipment in a news-report can have serious implications. For example, reports that tanks and not armoured personnel carriers, infantry carrying vehicles are being used in counter insurgency operations in 'Aid to Civil Authorities' could create alarm the world over. And, 'media-savvy' Public Relation Officers down to a unit / sub-unit level, must be appointed, since the battlefield of tomorrow will be that of low-intensity conflicts and of **limited wars** (emphasis added), where higher formation headquarters will often be too far away to respond quickly to the demands of the media."

"A key issue that senior Military officers in most armies, are yet to come to terms with, is that while the widest reach is that of the electronic media, it is paradoxically also the most superficial in its content. So, a long drawn out interview is often a waste of time with TV journalist, who will often carry only a sound-byte or two. News on TV is about the understated narrative, the accumulation of fact and images, that make the case more strongly than any argument. And, in TV, a subject makes news for about six hours, after twelve hours it is often history. Also, TV crews often prefer to show younger and more energetic commanders on the ground, who look good and sound good. The print media prefers to meet senior officers for detailed interviews which are **quoted verbatim** (emphasis added). Both have their own importance. The shelf life and reference value of printed matter is much higher than a TV report, and it thus requires equal attention."

"It is important to understand that for the media 'bad news is good news and good news is no news', and whether it is Kosovo, Kargil or Kandhar, it is the media's job to report the news and it is what they will continue to do. And this could happen with greater frequency than ever before, with round the clock news channels mushrooming everywhere. But these often lack in quality reporting, since more could mean worse. And so, journalists in the field will be under pressure from their news editors to give 'consumer-oriented news', with pre-conceived notions. But good journalists are always objective. The fourth estate or the media is on nobody's side, the more professionally they are dealt with, the more **positive is their response** (emphasis added)."

"While analysis can be left to the columnists, a reporter attempts to show the situation on the ground, who is doing what to whom, and with what effects and why. As the media has its eyes and ears to the ground, it can be said that when there is a policy vacuum, when Governments are without a course to follow or an expedient to clutch at, then newspaper or TV images have a jolting effect, goading the leadership to move on. Therefore, in the news business, it isn't indifference but involvement that makes all the difference. As commitment is essential to be a good soldier, good journalism is the 'journalism of attachment'."

Brig Mohan Bhandari, Brigadier General Staff, 15 Corps

"A very peculiar problem in Jammu and Kashmir and particularly the Valley which has caught the attention of the panel is the ability to interact with the local media. There are fifteen newspapers in vernacular being published in the Valley and this is a matter of serious concern to us. Somehow we have always talks of national hookups, the electronic media or the national dailies. The local media (in Kashmir Valley) is totally partial and do not think twice before publishing any malicious reports against the Army in particular, Security Forces and the **Nation in general** (emphasis added). The Kashmiris read local papers, mostly Urdu which carry very coloured versions of the incidents in the Valley on the front pages and the Army is invariably shown in poor light. To our surprise, we discovered that quite a few are on the payroll of interested parties."

"We also see that some of the national newspapers depict stories of Kashmir which are purely sensational. In fact, the daily achievements of the Security Forces are covered in a few lines only. No national newspaper publishes an Urdu version. The local Urdu newspapers are totally pro Pakistan. In most places in the vally the transmission of Doordarshan is not strong enough and people watch Pakistan TV and are exposed to anti national propaganda which tarnishes the image of Security Forces. Zee TV and Star TV channels are only available at Srinagar and Baramullah. There is the Kashish Channel which mainly broadcasts songs and dramas."

"Whenever there is a setback to the Security Forces the news is published in the headlines. In some papers three to four such articles are published, whereas successes of the Security Forces are given scant attention. Rebuttals by the Army are published on the last page which people normally do not read, whereas the onus is on the person who published the incorrect news."

Lt Gen HB Kala, PVSM, AVSM, SC, GOC-in-C ARTRAC

"Let us see what we should be doing:-

(a) The Ministry of Defence must lay down a policy on the subject because of the people involved.

(b) Functional relationship norms must be evolved to understand each other. Understand each other's domains keeping security considerations in mind.

Today these things are not existing but despite that we have been able to establish a very happy working relationship between the media and the Army as was witnessed in Kargil and that in itself is a great achievement. We are learning from our experience. What we have not achieved, as also the ground realities and working compulsions have been highlighted (in this seminar). We must be patient as we are working for a common aim and learning in the process and this must be accepted."

"As regards the Army being image conscious, why not. I am not apologetic for that. This has been ingrained in me as part of my service ethos. My counterpart a Secretary does not wear a uniform nor does an Editor-in-Chief of the Indian Express. I wear a distinct uniform. When I go to a particular institution the working environment changes."

"With all humility I ask the media whether they have that expertise. I have no expertise on media and have not been trained in media. By the same token, I request you to tell me if all your major newspapers, major TV networks which can throw away crores of rupees, or claim to have defence experts, have senior retired officers to help them. How many of them have sought professional assistance? Today one person is covering a number of beats, defence one day and municipal elections in Chandni Chowk the next."

Lt Gen OS Lochab, VSM

"During the Kargil war the world opinion tilted favourably towards India essentially due to the factor of transparency. However, during conflict situations, the transparency needs to be controlled to suit the requirements of military security. This has to be carefully monitored and tampered. During the initial stages of Kargil conflict, primarily due to safety reasons movements of journalists beyond Zojila was restricted. But with the passage of time and Army Liaison Cell having been restructured and ad hoc media cells having been created at Kargil, Srinagar and Udhampur, media personnel were sent up front. As you all know media briefings were held on a regular basis at Kargil and Srinagar. At Delhi a joint MoD – MEA briefing was held on daily basis. During a conflict a multi pronged strategy should be evolved, wherein various types of media are simultaneously addressed to educate the environment and enlarge the canvas of battlefield by bringing the war close to the masses. The electronic, print and cyber media must be carefully orchestrated at the conflict zone as also at the regional and national centres – for example discussions on the Kargil conflict and contemporary issues were telecast over a number of TV channels and net-chats organised by select media. During conflicts there is little time to educate media personnel on matters military. Journalists lacking basic understanding and knowledge of military organisations, tactics and military equipment may resort to speculative reporting. During the Kargil conflict the reporters could not go far ahead for more realistic reporting of infantry battles. The electronic media due to its heavy equipment, could not cover the infantry operations to the extent desirable. The media related infra-structure for transmission was not available at Kargil, because of which reports had to be couriered across Zojila to Srinagar leading to delays in reporting. The lesson thus learnt is that suitable logistics needs to be worked out and put in place at the very **beginning of any conflict** (emphasis added) to facilitate the movement and working of the media personnel."

"A synergetic approach is required wherein the Army and the media personnel work together towards a common goal. It is important for the media to keep the national interest uppermost in their minds and although activities of the Armed Forces can be highlighted and debated, norms of reporting must follow certain fundamental rules and guidelines so as not to harm the overall national cause. To ensure that smooth flow of information is maintained, various elements of Government and non-Government organisations need to be integrated. For example the Ministry of Information and Broadcasting may include members of the Armed Forces or MoD; like the MoD has PIB representatives through the DPR. Similar organisation may be created at various levels of interaction with media with professionals being integrated in the overall organisational structure. Thus, integration will help in formulating an integrated policy on media and terminal objective will be achieved with fair amount of accuracy."

Mr Prabhash Joshi

"Before coming here, yesterday I met Mr George Varghese, an old friend for last 20 years to discuss various aspects as he was a member of Su.brahmanyam Committee on Kargil and is one of the objective watchers of Indian media. Mr Varghese is amongst the top ten credible journalists in India. After long discussion with him I could conclude that Mr Varghese was not happy that Indian press and TV channels have not really deliberated on Kargil Report as he felt that proper discussion was not held on the subject. Mr Varghese said that it was for the first time in the whole world that certain aspects about the Armed Forces had been included which no other nation ever included in its reports to the media / public about its Defence Forces. He also felt that media did not take adequate interest in the report and probably it was due to the fact that no one was specifically blamed in he report and no political mileage thus could be derived out of it. As only military and security measures were included, press did not deliberate in detail. During the conflict we saw that press / electronic media had made available all details to homes of viewers through TV, but after the conflict it was not the same. If eminent people like Mr Varghese felt this, then I feel there is a reason to worry in the country. There is therefore a requirement as Indians to take interest in matters of military and security. Before Kargil, no war or conflict had reached homes of Indians whereas during Kargil people were keenly involved in the progress of operations. I felt both during the Gulf War and also during Kargil operations that the war tends to become a spectacle and market forces tend to **commercialise the war** (emphasis added). Thus media must ensure that war / conflict are not made into a spectacle by sensationalising as no country wants to go to war, it is only under some compulsion that nations go to war. Thus making of war as a spectacle on a TV leads public to see it as a cinema leading to **artificial sense of national pride** (emphasis added). In Nagaland, when body of a decorated soldier was taken for the last rites during Kargil operations, it was felt by the nation that Nagaland was very much a part of India by the immense turnout of locals and by the sense of national pride displayed by them. A large amount of compensation was given to the widows of soldiers who lost their lives during operation in Kargil, which was really a good thing. However, a lot of houses disintegrated as money was given only to the widows and nothing was paid to the parents of the individual. It is not only for the wife that a soldier earns for but also has the responsibility to look after his parents. Thus when such soldier dies in operations it is necessary that full amount of monetary compensation be not only given to the widow of the soldier but a portion be also earmarked for the **parents** (emphasis added). There is thus a need to ensure that the families of soldiers including their parents are looked after in case of demise of any soldier and not make it into a spectacle."

"For example, during the hijacking of Indian Airlines flight to Kandhar in the end of 1999, media made a spectacle of it by showing 50-60 families of the passengers on the TV time and again and thus creating undue pressure on the Government to look after the interests of these families vis-a-vis the national interests. This led to the release of militants very much against the interests of the nation. The pressure on the Government was only due to projecting of these 50-60 families over and over again by the TV channels. This can be termed as **good use of TV, as also as a bad use of TV** (emphasis added). In larger interest of the country it was necessary that the nation should not have surrendered to the demand of hijackers and deplored the handling by the media. TV should have ensured that such large-scale spectaclising of the situation should have been avoided. I know that tight control on this medium is not possible, however, I am surprised to note that there used to be a line of control in the print media as for the Defence Forces and it seems to be breaking down fast. Often I see that on serious reports given by reporters, adequate control is not available in the channels like chief sub, news editor, deputy editor and editor. In some cases editors come to know of contents only once they see the paper in the morning like any other common person. When I was a sub- editor, my editor/ publishers used to read the contents before publication of the paper in the night to avoid unwanted and embarrassing material/report being published. As in a case of my paper, a report got published that the Army is not capable of handling situation in Kashmir. This line did convey a very wrong perspective to the nation - as the whole country believes that Army is the only institution which can be effective when all others fail whether it is case of foreign aggression or in case of any likelihood of disintegration internally of the nation. I feel lot of people have more faith in the Army than even the Constitution of the country. Thus such reports about Army being published in the newspapers do create a wrong impression. I know the Army did not mean what was printed in the media."

"As means of communications and IT improve rapidly, we need to ensure that conflict and media need to be handled in a balanced manner to ensure that nation should not feel that correct details have not been made known to it and also nation should not feel that it has been let down. In a democracy it is necessary that media should be credible as also its institutions like the Constitution, Parliament and the Armed Forces should be credible. To make these institutions and more so the media credible, I feel that:-

(a) Armed Forces and media must have **greater interaction** (emphasis added). There are a large number of big newspapers that do not even have defence correspondents. I also do not know if our TV channels have some training for its reporters on defence matters.

(b) There were reports during Kargil operations that many reporters were lacking in skill about the background, defence equipment, tactics/strategy pertaining to the Defence Forces. This was due to lack of proper training of these reporters.

(c) Our reporters often lack objectivity and credibility due to tendency to sensationalise the issues.

(d) The communication available and liaison personnel of the Armed Forces with the media lack necessary speed, thus at times they are overtaken by events.

(e) If we are really concerned about national security we need to ensure that the nation is kept informed of security matters.

(f) **Media is a force multiplier** (emphasis added). This term I have heard in Kargil Committee Report and also in various seminars. The impact on public due to media is immense, but what is being actually published outside including how the war was fought is different. Soldier is not an actor and is not interested in what image of his is being projected outside. Soldier is more interested in his battle than the image. Thus media needs to be objective in ensuring image of the Armed Forces is kept in correct perspective. To ensure objectivity, credibility interaction between media and, the Defence Forces must be almost ***ten times*** of what it is today (emphasis added).

(g) I have no doubt that the press/media has the highest regards for the Armed Forces vis-a-vis any other institution of the nation. It was not that India won the media war but it was due to the **Army actions that Kargil War was won** (emphasis added). I feel that journalists and media personnel must lay more stress on professionalism than national interests while covering war like situations. Thus if I as a professional, have proper skills and can report objectively in the newspaper then I can serve the nation in a way similar to the soldier on the battlefront."

Mai Gen Ashok Mehta. AVSM. VrC (Retd}

"Kargil has brought to the fore the uneasy Media-Military relationship which has swung from conciliation in the late eighties to confrontation a decade later, ironically after the Army's recognition of the media being a **force multiplier** (emphasis added). The interaction between the two sides was reinvigorated in the mid-eighties so that each would become sensitive to the other's professional concerns. Unfortunately but not surprisingly, the adversarial relationship has come to stay. At times news making has ignored national security imperatives. Worse, conduct of military operations has been politicised and the media has taken sides on it. At the end of the Kargil war, the Chief of the Army Staff was forced to admit that while the military may have won the war on the ground it had **lost the Information War** (emphasis added). The lesson thus is that the Army has to create the capability to fight a two-front war."

"There's no doubt that the Army, like any other institution, has become sensitive to criticism. But unlike other institutions, its concerns involve the lives and morale of its soldiers. Even after Kargil, Kargil has become a no-holds-barred battle between the Military and the media. The Army has landed into controversy, some times because of its lack of aptitude in putting across its case, but most of the times, because it cannot defend itself with the same vigour if it is attacked due to organisational and operational constraints."

"Instead of forging a meaningful strategic partnership, they are becoming natural adversaries. Especially during operations -war, proxy war and counter insurgency – the two sides have to harmonise their sensitivities and concerns, with a media both putting and pulling the stops so that lives of soldiers are not endangered. So frustrated are some senior officers after the most recent controversy over the alleged shifting and loss of Point 5353 in Kargil that they are asking which is the lesser evil; **transparency or secrecy** (emphasis added)? And why the needless needling by the media? Only recently, the MoD in Britain took a journalist, Tony Geraghty, to task for breaches of the Official Secrets Act for his book, '*The Irish War*' which was said to have damaged military security and put to risk, lives of combatants, the author was blacklisted. *Harper and Collins* were asked to stop publication of the paperback edition, his contract as military consultant to television terminated and a claim of Pounds 170,000 pressed against him. There are fairly stable rules of voluntary censorship on covering the conflict in Northern Ireland. During the Falklands War, censorship was at source. Nearer home, the war in Sri Lanka is covered in a blanket of censorship, except for the foreign media. Ostensibly this is to protect the morale of the soldiers but is the other extreme."

"Not too long ago, there was a veil of secrecy over counter insurgency operations in the North East till human rights and civil rights activists exposed the excesses committed by the Army and violations of law."

"Hence, over time, the realisation and acceptance that good soldiering had to be within the norms of civilised behaviour and law of the land. Good relations with the media and observance of human rights have become integral to the command functions of every military commander as has factoring the force multiplication effect of the media in **winning the Information War** (emphasis added). At the end of the day, what is at test is the credibility of the Army as well as the credibility of the media. In India, while the media is not fully informed to write on the Military, the latter, when at the receiving end, can scarcely defend itself."

"Building a Fruitful Relationship. The question is how does one build a fruitful relationship? Clearly, there is no cut and dry solution but there is need for each side to appreciate and respect the other's strength and weakness. Despite years of trying to bridge this perception gap, there is inadequate understanding of the media by the Military and vice-versa. Some reporters say it is pointless criticising the media for not comprehending the ethos of the Army because it never will. Instead the Military should understand the way newspapers and magazines are structured and identify levels of intervention when things go wrong."

"Similarly, there is a view in the Army that they have a job to do and as long as they are killing the enemy efficiently, it is all that matters. Neither view is correct. The question has to be asked whether the media has a role in promoting and protecting national security. The events of the last two years, whether it be the dismissal of Admiral Bhagwat or the removal of Brig Surinder Singh or the most recent controversy over Point 5353, would show otherwise. All these cases were needlessly politicised and showed the Army, which is fighting a proxy war, in bad light. Media intervention did not reflect any sensitivity over security slippages."

"In the case of Brig Surinder Singh, the same combination of players (lawyers, opposition politicians and the media) sought to make him a hero when he was a villain. Nobody had heard of a hill called Point 5353 (denoting its height in meters) till a journalist reported last month that though it belonged to India, it had been lost to Pakistan during the Kargil War. Maps and facts were falsified to make this claim and despite an official rejoinder that Point 5353 was never in Indian possession, nor on the Indian side of the L of C, the media persisted in challenging the Army's contention by giving it a different spin. Doubting the veracity of reports put out by the Army has become routine. The media at one time was even challenging the Army's **figures of casualties in Kargil** (emphasis added)."

"Point 5353 was resurrected two weeks ago at an elaborate media briefing held at a five star Delhi hotel by famous criminal lawyer, Mr RK Anand. He produced classified operational documents to challenge the Army's claim that Point 5353 had not been lost to Pakistan, thereby implying the Army had been lying. If Mr Anand had only bothered to heed the Army's earlier rejoinder, he would have known that as per authenticated maps exchanged after the Shimla Agreement, Point 5353 lies on the LoC."

"In the encounter with Mr RK Anand, the Army was forced to reveal certain information, which in national interest should have remained under **wraps** (emphasis added). Funnily, Pakistan was prompt to report that it had not violated the Line of Control in Kargil. The media being inveigled into motivated controversy is inimical to healthy **Military-Media relations** (emphasis added)."

"Goof ups by the Military. All this is not to say the Services do not have their share of goof ups. The list is long and starts with the Rodrigues fiasco (the Army Chiefs 1993 interview with the 'Pioneer'), Chrar-e-Sharief (1994), the IAF revolt in 1995, the publication of the Kashmir Diary by Lt Gen Arjun Ray, the Bhagwat saga and the Kargil war.

"It seems the Army especially learnt no lessons from its mishandling of these incidents. It acted with too little defence too late. It took up with the Press Council of India, some cases against journalists reporting the **Kargil war** (emphasis added), notably Brig Surinder Singh's case, but received no relief from the Press Council at that time, prompting an officer to say that when a soldier makes a mistake he's immediately penalised but when a journalist does so, he goes scot-free."

"Despite its limited and truncated powers the Press Council, in its recent order, has rapped '*Outlook*' magazine for creating letters written by Brig Surinder Singh to higher ups in the Army during the Kargil war. Worse, the Press Council says the magazine did not bother to report the Army's point of view, even when the Army wrote to them, thus ignoring the basic canon of good journalism -free and fair reporting."

"The Army errs on the side of caution in order not to antagonise the media. Many of the Kargil-related problems would have been nipped in the bud if it had had a formal system for the immediate rebuttal of mis-reporting and aggressively pursued the **source of the story** (emphasis added). Even when it acted, it goofed up as in the case of summons issued to journalists for a court of inquiry in the Brig Surinder Singh's case that was contrary to existing instructions on summoning civilian witnesses."

"The media has become both aggressive, assertive and investigative in its reporting but without the necessary focus. It still prefers subjects like arms deals etc. The military has to realise it cannot hide 'bad news'. And the media, that it cannot 'concoct news'. Antagonists can become **partners too** (emphasis added)."

"In the end I suggest that proprietors and editors of the media must get involved in seminars like this to understand the problems instead of junior reporters as they are the ones in actual command. Mr Arun Jaitley, Minister of I & B must chair the meeting with proprietors and editors and work out rules of business of news reporting and aspects of national security that have an impact on operations and lives of soldiers."

Mr Arnab Goswami

"Gen Mehta as regards the point you made, I share some of the disappointments that I was not around in 1984 but I share the disappointment if indeed it is the case, this is an issue which is discussed again and again and again. But I would differ with you in the analysis that this issue is being discussed again and again in the Army or the Army does not understand the media. In fact I think this issue is being discussed again and again because the Army understands the media **too well** (emphasis added)."

"The first characteristic that I have learnt about journalists when they are in a group is that they have a certain behavioural pattern. If I sit in front of a senior Army officer and I have to get a favour from him or any privilege from him alone in a room, I will plead with him. If you invite me to his room with four to ten other journalists of about my same seniority and somewhat similar background and you discuss the same situation, I will negotiate with him. But if you bring me in a situation where I am sitting with 50 plus journalists in a crowded room or a press conference and then discuss the same situation with you, then I will make a speech. So if your sit alone, I will plead with you; I sit with a few people, I will negotiate, and if you put me in a room as big as this and so many journalists around and one senior Army officer talking of a situation or giving a press briefing, I will make a **speech** (emphasis added)."

"I will request you to look back at what was happening during the Kargil War and the reference was there to the joint MoD / MEA briefing. I remember distinctly to have gone for about 14-15 of those briefings myself as a person on the spot covering the situation in Delhi and I used to come back and say you see first we never got a turn to speak and we used to very often end up listening to our fellow colleagues making speeches, giving their analysis of the situation, exhorting the Army to do something and not asking any serious question. Now, I find it surprising that this is the one issue, which has not been asked so far, that is the media asking any serious question at all of the Army? Or have we become habituated to a situation where we make speeches, feel important, go into the battlefield, sit in a bunker, refuse to acknowledge that we are sitting in a bunker, take a handout and at the end of the day make ourselves heroes whether it is in a press conference or in that bunker rather than ask any serious question of the Army."

"So, I just like to begin with my first submission to all of you is that far from being adversarial the **media has been far far pliant** (emphasis added). In-fact, just last month I re-read a book on what had happened in

Gulf War, it is called "Second Front" and all of you must have read it at one stage or another and it describes how pliant the American media had been at that point of time. I always try to look back and see how we were behaving during the Kargil War and since the subject is national security how we were behaving during Kandhar. I think we were being far too pliant. When this question was raised earlier in the day that when the protests were taking place outside PM's house by the families of passengers of the hijacked Indian Airlines plane, why was TV covering it? You were basically going against national security and forcing the Government to a corner and you are not supposed to do that; but you at the end of the day were part of the compromise. I think that is wholly unfair thing to say. If I was in TV and you were one of those remotely connected to the situation of hijacking and your brother/sister/father was standing outside PM's office and not even Central Secretariat talking about that situation, protesting about not getting adequate information and if I as part of TV was not covering it, you think I would be doing my job, I do not think do. That really is the definition of my job that I keep for myself, which is why that point Mr Joshi made and he is far more distinguished than me and has complete right to make it; is very true that if it comes to this that you put professionalism and patriotism before me, I will choose to be a professional first and do not grudge me for it because I am doing **my job** (emphasis added)."

"Well, we are living in a country and issue of Point 5353 was raised by Gen Ashok Mehta. Now let us also understand the kind of country we are living in - we live in a country where one person can be a criminal lawyer one day, pay some money to a political party and become a Rajya Sabha MP the next day, next day dole out cash and sit in a Five Star Hotel and hold a press -conference on a big security lapse -like Point 5353. He was a criminal lawyer one-day but before the end of weekend he was a military strategist. It is shocking that this should be happening. But at the same time consider how many times during the Kargil War did you ever see any serving senior Army officer sitting with Mr Prannoy or me or in any of our programmes and **telling the country what was happening** (emphasis added). You see it is a huge advantage to have some one like Gen Ashok Mehta, who has seen both sides of the fence and call him to my studio, I know I am getting that perspective also; he is sympathetic to both sides and gives me the correct picture. But it will be still better if I had one of you sitting in my studio talking about the situation. Why is the feeling that if a senior General comes to the studio and says you see Mr Arnab on that question he will have no comments because that compromises national security? Why is there a sense then that I will keep probing him on it, trying to put him in a corner, refuse to acknowledge that there are some shared concerns that the media has with the Army, why is that an assumption that media is out there to only sensationalise, **it is not true** (emphasis added). Believe me, it is not true and I will give you an example since we are on the subject and I want to keep shifting between the subject of national security and the Army because it is one linked subject."

"We should trust the media little more, I think they know their job. It is all right when you go to a front area and then you go with an escort and you do not decide which unit to go to. You go to the commanding officer, he tells his junior officer to take you to an area and bring you back: that is all right. But it is not as irresponsible as that and I must make a point that in the future if we have situations like Kargil or any such - we must have more of the Government/more of the Army sitting in our studios than letting us speak or doing the talking or doing the speculating or doing the talking with people who are not experienced and be **blamed for all of that later** (emphasis added)."

"One of the points that was made was about national interests, I have severe problem with this **definition of national interests** (emphasis added). I am from the North East and my father who has been a Colonel with the Madras Sappers and has served in Nagaland, we know the situation there - how bad it is. Now, I can tell you without any hesitation that the Chief Minister of Nagaland is in league with the militants and if somebody tells me that respect the democratically elected Government, do not jeopardise it or do not say anything that will compromise it completely - if I say that democratically elected Government won the elections in a situation when not even an independent was fighting that election because the gun happened to be on their side. And if I am a journalist in Nagaland and I don't respect that Government, can I be blamed for it? Which side of the story do I give then? I would like to give the

Army's point of view because they are not meant to be there, they have been assigned a complicated job of combating the insurgency. But at the same time I would also tell that these are the people who say that well, this is happening, that is happening, cease-fire is being breached on both sides. I think I have to do my job."

"I also think there is a problem with taking patriotism a little too far. You see the Gulf War started on a rumour that 300 premature children were pulled out by Saddam Hussain almost personally from the incubators and left to die on the cold streets of Baghdad. It was a rumour - Amnesty International without verifying it had gone by that rumour and it had become the single biggest focal point of this big American campaign to suddenly demonise Saddam Hussain. The person who till a week back had met five senior American Congressmen, a delegation sent by George Bush, where he was looked as greater friend than Khomeini, had suddenly become a dictator and gone to war with America on the basis of a rumour that 300 Iraqi or Kuwaiti children were left to die by this horrible man who had. removed the incubators and left them to die. Later on it was not found to be true. In retrospect, the whole of America asked itself the question that did we verify what was said? Who said it? And it turned out the rumour had been started off by the daughter of the Kuwaiti ambassador to America who had appeared before an American Congress Committee and had said that 300 children had died in the incubators because Saddam Hussain had removed incubation machines. Rumour carried too far thus can have a reverse effect and I do not mean this with any disrespect. If we have glamourised war, made it out part of marketing mechanism -then yes it has. Let us not forget it that during the war the TV channels came anywhere close to the entertainment channels in terms of viewer ship. But, I would just like to ask you, there were a thousand and one rumours during the Kargil War itself which could have been **exploited** (emphasis added) but we did not need that kind of pop-patriotism to keep Kargil alive and I am sure there were enough soldiers or professional fighting there who knew their job – we did not need **Coke and Pepsi kind of campaign** (emphasis added) to sustain Kargil or achieve what we did. It goes a bit too far when all you see are the good images, now it is being asked but they may not have been asked during Kargil – we are very safe journalists we do not want to lose our sources so some journalists who did not want to lose his source during the 1965 War did not give out the story that is coming out now."

"When Vikram Batra became a martyr and some one gave the story later that how he had said '*Yeh dil maange more*', taking off on a soft drink commercial. Did anybody verify that? Did anybody hear him say that? How many people were there as real witnesses to what was said and what was not said? If that story was said by some one why did it become a national event, why did the first line of a national news bulletin not lead with the number of casualties or what had happened in the war but started off with this catchy slogan. Do we want to see this kind of pop - patriotism coming out in the future? I think if we don't, then we should have some real reporting. In the next conflict when it happens, the Generals should be out there giving the story and there will be no speculation and there will be **real respect for them** (emphasis added). In the next conflict there should be some unilateral reporting. It is all right to take some pool of journalists out there, some body has a better access with cellular telephones and goes with the story first but I think this pool system has **not worked at any point of time** (emphasis added). And I think, in next conflict it may be that a reporter can be trusted a little more to be sent a little bit more to the forward area that is if he/she is keen about it. If he / she is willing to risk his life then that I think is real patriotism. When you are going out with our soldiers, it is not patriotism when you count the number of dead / who have come back and make yourself the **hero as a result of that** (emphasis added)."

"Also, you see the Army has looked too much at traditional ways of interacting with journalists. One of them I believe that there is some provision by which a journalist of some years of experience can go and spend three months with the Army / Navy / Air Force to have a sense of what is happening. I think it is only a feel thing – I feel if the Army continues to look at the Press in such a way i.e. next time a reporter goes with me then he is a good reporter, if he dresses in the same way and talks in the same way, is as disciplined as me and has the same sense of professionalism or the national pride / duty as me then it will not be the right thing. A journalist is **different** (emphasis added); he has opted for this profession and one should let him do his job. Interaction can happen at much more honest form than this little jaunt that everybody has taken. I know journalists are famous for looking for junkets – I think there can be better junkets than this."

"About peacetime operations, I think that is where you can actually make the media feel involved, the **country feel involved** (emphasis added). Mr Saeed Naqvi is not here today, I watched his programme "World Report" and this was about an infantry unit going to Middle-Eastern country and I recognised an officer who was giving a brief to the reporter on what happened there when his unit reached. The officer was of the rank of Lieutenant, a youngster; he was so good with what he was saying, actually felt proud that this 23 year old is so proud to tell what he was doing. My point is why cannot you **trust your own people a bit more** (emphasis added). If a youngster comes to the camera and tells what he did for the country -what is the harm? Why this insulation? If you want to involve the country more, do not make these youngsters TV celebrities but allow them to come out a little more. This closed door approach, I think must change in someway."

"Another point I would like to make is the problem of access; you cannot enter Army HQ without a PIB card. You cannot talk to anyone to get the information required. You will not get information on regular basis, as there is no regular interaction. When something happens in J&K, I will tell another correspondent there to get details, some Army officers will give some inputs and others will not. But if there were a regular interaction as in case of Kargil War this **problem would never have risen** (emphasis added). I think so many problems / speculation can go, if little bit of openness is allowed. So instead of having a pool for journalists, I think there should be a pool of Army people who should be talking to the press regularly, **I mean this very seriously** (emphasis added)."

"During Kargil I was covering the Congress Party as also the MoD/ MEA briefings. I know what Mr Natwar Singh was saying in Congress briefings and what Col Bikram Singh was saying in joint briefings of MoD/ MEA. There was a world of difference in what the two were saying. My point is, do not let the politicians latch on to a situation; do not let them hog the limelight. I think some times that it is completely obscene that I do a panel discussion with Mr Mani Shankar Aiyar or Mr Ajit Jogi talking about Kargil. I do not think it should be happening. But please understand why I am being forced to do it because none of you will come. I think if the Army briefings drag a little bit many senior officers can come. Believe me no more questions will be asked of you if the reply is 'no comments'."

"I am saying it again, , do not want to be apologetic about it, and during the Kargil War we searched for the information in a great way. First time Gen Arjun Ray came to our office was 15-20 days after the war had already started, by then speculation had already taken place, complications had happened, rumours were already ripe. Why could not he have come earlier and briefed us. Let me be honest no journalist is interested in nitty-gritty of what the Army is doing, a journalist only wants to make a **hero out of himself** (emphasis added). If you come and debrief me in my coffee - room in the NDTV, it will not help me. It helps really if you come and talk before the TV camera."

"I do not want to be very negative about the whole thing but again we are in a very commercial medium and our ratings are very bad after '*Kaun Banega Crorepati*' came in, we have been routed. So, the next time there is a whiff of a conflict, I am saying this with all seriousness; the whiff of a difficult situation; next time I see that masked man sitting with Home Secretary talking about peace in Kashmir; I will just latch on to it. I will discuss it for 15 days on my programme and I will show those videos again and again because I have to sell my channel. And, everybody sold his or her channel during Kargil conflict. Nobody did any exclusive story. Everybody carried the same story – **based on pop-patriotism** (emphasis added). On slightest whiff of conflict – why did everyone latch on to the Point 5353, we were missing that action and thought it had come again. Let the Army know that the media can be made a friend very quickly if you talk to them regularly, if you interact with them regularly and come on their programme and be honest about it and tell them your limitations. Do not wait for the next conflict to **recount our same experiences again and again** (emphasis added).

Mr Ram Mohan Rao

"Firstly, politicians are interested to remain in power, if they do not remain in power the purpose is not served. In a parliamentary democracy if they do not discuss in the Parliament the 'Kargil Report' thread bare or discuss fine points of security then it does not mean that our parliamentarians are not interested in national security. They are certainly interested in national security and if you look at the Kargil period of conflict, it was the Government, which had lost its virtual majority in the parliament; it gave the Armed Forces or the Army full discretion how to fight the war without any kind of **day-to-day interference** (emphasis added). And whenever national security required some action to be taken they took that action."

"If you look at the Kargil Report and see the mistakes that occurred or immediately after that why did they not discuss but appointed a committee. Also, remember they were facing elections, if you want to bring out faults about the Army, Air Force or the Navy or about officers at that time, of course politicians will use that to attack those in power when they are going for re-election. I think, then such reports will only be discussed later when the tempers are down. Therefore, I think there is no reason to fault the Government on that aspect. The Kargil Report was published, there were many operations earlier and we do not know the facts about them, certain **deletions** (emphasis added) were made in the Kargil Report. Who were responsible for making those deletions? I think many of us who were sitting in chairs where you make decisions, we felt that if these pieces of information are given out it will help the enemy and compromise our sources. Basically all that was necessary for the country to know was published but what can compromise security was not included. It was **not an over-secretive document** (emphasis added)."

"There was also this remark made that it should be decided at the highest level of the Government to be transparent. Mind you, I have had the opportunity to interact at the highest level of the Government with the Armed Forces, with the civil services and with the politicians. There are rules on the subject, which allow us to be **transparent** (emphasis added). The Government at the highest level i.e., the Emergency committee of the Cabinet in 1967 had laid down and today they are available in form of Army Orders and also directives to the people who are charged with job of disseminating information. If you want to share that information, the rules do not prevent you. Yes, an individual minister or cabinet may decide at that level that they will not share particular information due to its various implications. But, it is not that there is no provision for it. If we decide at the Army or Governmental level what information can be given out, then in the system a concerned person should go up to the higher authority and explain what needs to be given out. Again, if you look back at Kargil, *except for the first two weeks when we stopped the media from going there*, but even then the media that was already there was not thrown out but remained there and there was no censorship. Afterwards there was an **attempt to share information** (emphasis added). So, again a mistake was done, we did not put in place a system for which guidelines exist of sharing information with the pressmen who were at Dras, Kargil, Srinagar. Where as a fairly good system existed at Delhi for briefings. So, if we want to do anything there are provisions, there are rules and our system allows that to happen and each one of us are senior enough and part of the Government to be able to **share information**" (emphasis added).

"There is this always - other talk about how the press does not understand national interests and they are patriots or non-patriots or professionals or non- professionals as Mr Arnab Goswami brought out. Something on which I have reservation about. Yes, all of us are professionals and we have a task, a job to do. All of us are patriots too being citizens of this country .We also have responsibility while we are citizen of the country and it is our own judgement how we carry out the responsibility. Newspapers and channels have to sell themselves to make them heard or feel and how they do it is also a difficult task. Newsman is looking for information or stories or bytes as the audio-visual media talks. They are looking for hard news, they are looking for human-interest stories and please remember there will always be people who want to sensationalise. If a bit of information is there that can be re-written and presented as headline in sensational manner, they will do it. And do not ever think that you can **discipline the whole lot** (emphasis added). There will always be one person who will sensationalise and my experience has been if it is something highly secret which affects national security, which affects Government's policy at a very sensitive level then do not share that information. You expect that the person with whom you are sharing that information might give it out and if he does give it out don't hold it against him, because he is doing his job and I do not know what pressures are there for him to do it that way. But if you think that you cannot take that risk do not then take that risk."

"Lastly, Mr Shekhar Gupta yesterday said, "do not use the word media- management, you do not manage the media". But I would put it slightly differently **media-management has a different connotation** (emphasis added). Dissemination of information, interacting with the media is also a professional job and you should know how newspapermen functions, who does what kind of story, when you are disseminating information whom are you talking to? Are you talking to an editor? Are you talking to a Chief of Bureau? Are you talking to a special correspondent? Are you talking to a reporter? If you know these things you will realise, you will get a certain thing, you can expect a certain report to appear in the newspaper or not to appear. A highly analytical piece of information, if you give it to a reporter it is of not much use to him as he will not be able to write that story as his editor will not accept such information from his reporter. I have also had the experience of politicians / bureaucrats / senior people in the Army calling only editors out as they will only want to deal at that level. Editors come, meet, share your whisky, go back and not write anything. They only write editorials or edit page articles, but if you are expecting something to appear in a newspaper you must call a correspondent and speak to him. If you are calling a person from audio-visual media, you will not only have to give him a story but also visuals to illustrate that story. The Armed Forces personnel or the bureaucrats thus must know intimately how the **media functions** (emphasis added) and if among you there is someone who is interested in professional aspects of dissemination of information or public relations or liaison work with the media, please learn this as it is a professional job and not an amateur's job."

Appendix D

The Media in Pakistan

In 1947, Pakistan inherited a press with a tradition of defiance. Several newspapers which commenced publication in the Forties played a historic role in mobilising support for the independence movement, in the face of persecution and repression. Among these newspapers were *Dawn*, *Jang*, *Pakistan Times*, *Nawa-e-Waqt* and *Morning News*. In fact, Mohammed Ali Jinnah, the founder of Pakistan, took a personal interest in the publication of *Dawn*, making it an influential voice of the freedom movement.

Political instability, following the death of Quaid-e-Azam, had serious consequences for the freedom of the press. Even before the imposition of Martial Law in 1958, the press had begun to be manipulated by powerful bureaucrats, had the print media was subjected in bandages and hardships. The first victim of the first Martial Law was Progressive Papers Ltd., which was taken over by the military regime in 1959. Its publications included the liberal and outspoken *Pakistan Times*. The government strengthened its hold on the press with the promulgation of the Press and Publications Ordinance 1963, virtually ending the limited freedom the press enjoyed. Besides, the government took over the management of some of the leading national Urdu and English newspapers and journals under the umbrella of National Press Trust created by the establishment. In spite of continuous protests by journalists and publishers through the decades, it took until 1988 for the ordinance finally to be replaced by Repeal of the Press and Publications Ordinance (RPPO).

Source: "Essential Data on Pakistan", *Pakistan Almanac 2000-2001* (Karachi:Royal Book Company, 2001), pp. 429-432.

In spite of a hostile environment prevailing during successive governments, the press continued to grow, both nationally and regionally. Newspapers in Pakistan are published in Urdu and English, as well as in Sindhi, Gujrati and Pushto. The press exercises influence disproportionate to its circulation which remains limited due to low literacy levels. And while Urdu newspapers have far wider circulation, the English press is more influential because it is read by policy-makers.

Freedom of the press received a further setback with the imposition of Martial Law in 1977. The military regime clamped pre-censorship on the press, following the cancellation of the general elections scheduled for October. When newspapers editors began to leave blank spaces to indicate censored portions, this witty gesture of protest became a punishable offence under Martial Law. Several publications were banned, and for journalists were threatened with flogging for defying Martial Law Regulations.

Newspaper publishers explored other means to secure readership. Technological innovation was to play its part. Urdu newspapers, which were calligraphed by hand, began to switch to computerised composing, colour printing was introduced in the major newspapers and more attention began to be paid to the layout and appearance of a newspaper and graphic designers began to be employed. Today, the print media has caught up with worldwide developments in communications, with computerization, use of electronic mail, Internet and the latest printing technology.

The lifting of Martial Law in 1985 brought some relief to a battered press. It became truly free after the elections of 1988. Although Benazir Bhutto's elected government proved to be fairly tolerant of a vigilant and far from muzzled press, the press itself demonstrated that having survived Martial Law it could not be intimidated by politicians. In a democratic system, the threat persisted from armed militants of political and religious group, who could not bear criticism, attacking several newspaper offices and journalists. The growing trend towards investigative journalism has also led to several key figures in government filing (with varying justification) libel suits against journalists and newspapers – usually protracted or settled out of court.

The press's newfound resilience ensured that the process of development did not slow down. Several new publications began to compete for an overall readership that was hardly growing, especially for the English language press. The Urdu press has made headway in the print media by vastly enlarging the number of newspapers and journals with increasing readership. Besides the standard of journalism and production has also been consistently improving. The Sindhi language press alongwith growing circulation kept pace with times by innovative measures in the quality of contents and production to ensure the desired appeal and impact.

With the revival of political activities in the late 80's, there has been remarkable upsurge in the number of newspapers and magazines with wider circulation both in Urdu, English and Sindhi languages.

The press in the country is categorised into two groups, namely metropolitan and regional newspapers, mainly for regulating the terms of employment and wages for newspaper's workers and for the share government sponsored advertisements. Quite a good number of metropolitan (national newspapers in Urdu and English are simultaneously published for more than two cities.

Among the leading newspapers in this category are the Daily Jang (Urdu) is published from Karachi, Lahore, Rawalpindi, Quetta and London.

The Daily Nawa-i-Waqt (Urdu) from Lahore, Karachi, Rawalpindi/ Islamabad and Multan.

The Daily Khabrain (Urdu) is published from Lahore, Karachi, Islamabad, Multan, Sheikhupura and Muzaffargarh (AK).

The Daily Naya Akhbar (Urdu) from Lahore, Islamabad and Multan.

The Daily Wifaq (Urdu) from Lahore, Rawalpindi, Sargodha and Rahimyar Khan. The Daily Pakistan (Urdu) from Lahore and Islamabad.

The Daily Deyani (Urdu) is published from Karachi and Sukkur.

The Daily Paigham (Urdu) from Lahore, Faisalabad and Sahiwal.

The Daily Tijarati (Urdu) from Lahore, Gujranwala, Sargodha and Quetta.

The Daily Juraat (Urdu) from Lahore, Rawalpindi/Islamabad and Muzaffarabad. The Daily Masawat (urdu) from Lahore and Faisalabad.

The English language newspapers simultaneously published from two or more centres in the country are the Daily Dawn from Karachi and Lahore ; the management is planning to start its edition from Islamabad sometimes in March 2001.

The Daily Nation comes out from Lahore and Islamabad.

The Daily News International is published from Karachi, Lahore and Islamabad. The Daily Frontier Post, from Peshawar and Lahore.

Apart from the newspapers mentioned above there are many Urdu and English language newspapers that are published at various centres of the country.

They're about 10 newspapers being published in Sindhi language. The leading daily Newspapers from among them are Hilal-e-Pakistan, Wahedat, Kawish, Ibrat, Aftab, Singh News and Mehran.

The list of newspapers and journals which are the members of All-Pakistan Newspapers Society is given on page 433 (not reproduced here). There are many more newspapers and magazines that are not represented on the APNS.

There is an official organisation under the Ministry of Information and Media development which ascertains the circulation of the newspapers and magazines through a system of audit, but with the varying figures of print order from time to time it is difficult to give exact figures. According to general estimates the total number of Urdu newspapers' circulation is about two million and the combined English newspapers' circulation is about 200,000.

News Agencies

There is a well organised network of local and foreign news agencies operating in the country. The Associated Press of Pakistan is the major news network under the government management. The APP, besides having its own offices and stringers for news collection within the country and abroad, has arrangement with foreign news agencies for news coverage, notably with Reuters, UPI and DPA etc.

The local news agencies namely Pakistan Press International (PPI), United Press of Pakistan (UPP) and National News International (NNI) operate in the private sector.

Press Organisations

The people associated with the print media in the country have different representative bodies with the objective of regulating the industry and safeguarding their respective interests. The All-Pakistan Newspapers Society (APNS) is the body of owners of publications; Council of Pakistan Newspapers Editors (CPNE) a representative body of take care of code of conduct and allied issues; the Pakistan Federal Union of Journalists; the All-Pakistan Newspaper Employees Confederation (APNEC), a federating organisation to protect the right of press workers. These press bodies operate on national scale. There are many other unions of journalists representing their region, cities and town which function as bargaining agents to protect their rights and establish harmonious relationship with their respective management's of press industry.

Electronic Media

An efficient and modern media is essential for the economic, social and political development of country particularly for developing countries like Pakistan. In fact, it is an important organ of governance in the country. The present government has given due importance to this sector. Electronic media consists of Pakistan Broadcasting Corporation and Pakistan Television Corporation Limited. These two corporations are playing effective role for socioeconomic uplift of the country and entertainment to the people.

At independence, Radio Pakistan had only two transmitters, in Peshawar and Lahore. Within two decades, eight stations were on air. Radio's role in the early years as a medium of information, education and entertainment was truly significant, specially in the absence of television and the prevalence of large-scale illiteracy which affected the circulation of newspapers. The number of sets increased phenomenally with the introduction of transistor radios. Radio Pakistan was converted into the Pakistan Broadcasting Corporation (PBC) in 1972. In 1997 there were 27 radio stations, covering 97.5 per cent of the population. The introduction of FM stations in the private sector has been tremendously a popular development, with its call-in programme formats.

Pakistan Broadcasting Corporation played a pivotal role in promoting national interest by providing information, entertainment and education to audiences at home and abroad. At present, PBC has 27 stations through out the country, including 3 FM stations at Islamabad, Lahore and Karachi with total transmitting power of 3721 kW in medium and short wave. The programme/news are now broadcast for 442 hours a day, 392 in home, which includes 85 hours of FM service and 50 in world and external services. At present, 21 foreign radio stations are monitored in seven languages by PBC Central News Organization.

Pakistan Television (PTV) started transmission with two stations in 1964. By the Nineties it was broadcasting from five cities. With satellite transmission and rebroadcast stations, it covered about 85 per cent of the population. PTV's second channel, introduced by satellite transmission on Asiasat, covers thirty-eight countries in South Asia and the Middle East, and is aimed at Pakistan's substantial expatriate community, especially in the Persian Gulf. PTV has come a long way from a few hours of live broadcasts of programmes in the initial years to technically sophisticated productions and 24-hour transmission. Its programmes are not only in the national language, Urdu, but in English and in most regional languages.

Pakistan Television Corporation Limited established in 1967 with the prime objectives and functions to establish a Television Network in the country for the provision of television broadcast services by telecasting programmes of al kinds i.e., news, pictorial, documentaries, local and foreign films for the purpose of disseminating information, education and purposeful entertainment. There are two channels in the country, namely, General Purpose Television (PTV-1) and Second TV Channel for Education (PTV-2). In addition, PTV has also obtained right to use air time to SRBC 13 transmitters on income sharing basis.

Introduction of PTV-WORLD towards the utilization of facilities and commercial potential of PTV-2 has proved successful. It has developed its viewership and also commercial potential over a period of one year. It provides a second choice to the viewers and an advertisement venue to parties who cannot affords publicity of their products on PTV. 1. Introduction of Prime TV from Oslo and Mid-East time from UAE for PTV viewers in Europe and Middle East respectively, has enabled PTV to telecast TV signal to Pakistani expatriates and also complete with other channels to find its place in international markets.

Since 1st Sept 2000 yet another channel No.3 has been added in news and informative programme as well items of national interest.

The estimate number of TV, VCR sets in the country as on June 30, 1999, were 3,035 million and 0.136 million respectively. As on March 31, 2000, the TV and VCR sets are estimated to be 3.150 million and 0.136 million respectively. License fee collection of VCR and Dish antenna has been suspended in view of directives of the previous government. However, license fee collection ratio is about 47 per cent of the registered sets, which is expected to improve in view of privatization of License Fee Collection.

In 1989, the government set up another network, Shalimar Television Network (STN) in Karachi, Lahore and Islamabad. For the first time, prime time on a television network was contracted out to a private company; Network Television Marketing, which telecast privately, produced programmes on STN. The STN network now covers ten cities of Pakistan. The development of television in Pakistan also resulted in a mushroom growth of video production units in the private sector. Meanwhile, satellite dish antennae are breaking the boundaries of communication and of censorship, often to the government's dismay.

In terms of programming, a relatively liberal policy had evolved for entertainment programmes and Talk shows. However, PTV news bulletins continue to be propagandistic in content and tone, focusing on the activities of government functionaries rather than on events evaluated for their news value.

In quite different ways, the print and electronic media in Pakistan have made significant progress since Independence. Both have developed dramatically in terms of technology and in the choice they now offer their audiences. But while the electronic media's growth has been in terms of greater reach and coverage, the print media has emerged from the relatively short period of censorship to come into its own as an outspoken and independent voice.

Appendix E

Press Institute of India

A Brief Survey Of The Difficulties Experienced By Correspondents Covering The Indo-Pakistan Conflict-1971

Some visiting correspondents and a few of the permanent ones were asked informally about the facilities (or lack of them) provided by the Indian Government, its approach to information and publicity and the reasons for the kind of coverage we got abroad. From these conversations a general pattern of inadequacies and complaints emerges. Broadly these are some of the heads under which they crystallize: -

Gathering of News

"The facilities provided were the most primitive in any coverage – war or no war", said one correspondent.

The main theme of the argument was that the 147 corespondents had come from thousands or miles away to cover a war and that is exactly what they were not allowed to do for the first crucial week or more. They had to sit in Delhi waiting day after day to go to the front; promises were extended every day that they would be allowed to go.

When at last some of them did go, they were taken to a safe sector far from where 'action' was. If this was because of a matter of governmental policy, they should have been told so, before they left Delhi. An exaggerated concern about their 'safety' and 'comfort' had the opposite effect of what perhaps was intended.

Source: USICAFHR Collection I; Colonel Pyaralal Papers, Bundle 7, 'Survey of Difficulties Faced by Correspondents Covering the Indo-Pakistan Conlict 1971'.

They were hardened war correspondents (many of them), used to taking risks and being knocked about. But unless they have seen a bit of the war, their stories were bound to lack colour and conviction.

According to most of them, their counterparts in Pakistan, were getting first-hand experience and their papers were crying out for similar stories. What they were getting from India were colourless, dull, rehashes of official communiqués.

Then again, their time at Delhi, while they waited to go to the front was idle. If the Government could not take them to the front quickly what they may have done was –

(a) To arrange some interviews here (with Pakistani infiltrators, some airmen and jawans returning from battle, such politicians and military officers as could be made available) to expose them to some direct 'action' through men actually involved. Pictures of these men should have been available.

(b) The PIB should have arranged a war room or a map room where a competent military officer could with the help of flags explain the latest situation, within the limits of security.

(c) Political scientists, experts in Indo-Pakistan relations, those with knowledge of the Kashmir case, geographers and a host of others – not necessarily Government officials but academicians – should have been available for groups to question them about the background.

(d) In general, an attempt should have been made to get across the idea that this war was a part of a larger problem.

This would have kept waiting newspapermen busy, given them something concrete to do and helped them to put whatever little they got from Government sources in a better context. After all, as one of them said, "Here was an unprecedented army of reporters from all over the world. Why not sell them your ideas and angles? You would have convinced some, removed biases, if any, of others."

Briefings

Most people felt that briefings were deftly handled by the Government spokesmen but they left much to be desired. At the briefings and from the Government communiqués only a guarded confirmation of action, which had concluded 24 hours or more earlier, was available. Specific questions asking for more details could not, naturally, be handled by a civilian spokesman of the Defence Ministry. Since most people were not allowed to get first-hand information from the front, which was imperative, these briefings could have had more depth and more meat. Rarely were any military or diplomatic briefings given.

The absence of detailed maps was, to a man, lamented. There were no maps-at the briefings (the ones produced a few times were not of much use). It should have been realised that getting good maps is difficult in Delhi for any individual. The PIB issue of maps was inadequate, late and erratic. It was a combination of enforced operation from Delhi (in the first week or so), and cautious and inadequate briefings which got India poor coverage and display in foreign newspapers which were getting deep and full first-hand stories from Pakistan, often accompanied by good pictures. These naturally got prompt and better display.

Censorship

Any newspaperman in a situation like this would like to be told and would readily accept, that there is censorship. If so, he would like to be told in detail what are the basic "don'ts" of military security and that the censorship machinery would be just, equitable and swift. This would presume that censors competent to dispose of disputed copy finally, should have been working and available almost round the clock. But more than once correspondents were told that there is no censorship. Instances of their copy being lifted from the telegraph office for "censoring" meant delays between anything from a few hours to two days. This unexpected delay was enough to put the back up of any correspondent and because of the delay, contribute to non-publication. A dialogue between the news editors and the correspondents went on continuously about missing copy, mutilated copy, copy arriving in wrong order with some paragraphs, sentences or even pages missing. Most correspondents would have preferred to voluntarily go and get their copy censored and cleared if they knew of a set-up for censorship existing. Another point made by many was that censorship at advanced basis like Jammu, Amritsar and Sialkot was slow and copy had often to be sent for further screening at Delhi.

Transmission of News

By and large everybody praised the functioning of the Telegraph offices. But for delays imposed by censors, copy was handled efficiently and promptly and other logistical details looked after very well. But the telegraph offices at Jammu and Amritsar, many felt, should have been strengthened by experienced staff. They appeared to be slow, indifferent and incompetent to deal with this tremendous rush of copy.

Pictorial and TV coverage

TV crews are cumbersome to handle but TV has enormous viewing and they should have been given priority to get authentic news. There are two TV agencies operating from Delhi. Through these a world audience was at India's doorstep.

What seems to have happened is that photographers (news and TV) were not allowed anywhere near operational areas (in the first week or ten days), the process of clearance and transmission was not made easy. Censorship was applied indiscriminately. Some pictures went through but oddly, a few got held up. Customs were extremely difficult to manage.

At a later stage, censorship demanded that TV films should be developed here and screened. For this there are no facilities in Delhi and even Bombay laboratories cannot efficiently handle some fast films. This meant enormous delay, worry and anxiety, wastage of energy (a man had to rush to Bombay, get films developed, come back to Delhi to screen them, etc) and the chance of the film being poorly developed, spoiling it for screening.

Even if all this was essential, censorship of films should have been arranged in Bombay to eliminate an additional trip to Delhi and delay.

Some TV cameramen complained of excessive caution, the army officers looking through the view, every time a shot was taken.

Press passes were often not recognized by policemen, involving wastage of time in chasing higher police officials. The time, which should have been spent in "shooting".

Press photographers, when eventually taken to the front, were confined to civil areas of bases like Amritsar, Ferozepur and Jammu. Those who went to the actual front, including Sikkim, a little later, were not given enough time to shoot.

The official pictures released were poor. They were 'dead' pictures, unimaginatively taken.

Trips to the Front

A delay of anything from 10 days to six was invariably reported between the time a request was made and it was granted. Requests to go to specific fronts were invariably not granted. Very often a paper had, say, the battle of Kashmir, or a particular part covered by its Pakistan correspondent and wanted its Indian correspondent to go to the same front to get a balanced and complete picture. But many asked for Lahore and got Jammu. This can be understood but the impression left on people was that this was due to conditions in the PIB rather than due to other inevitable compulsions. The passes to go to the front were rightly for a specified period, for 48 hrs, to a maximum of four days. But the journey (often 18 hours to Pathankot, then if lucky to Jammu) almost exhausted the time limit.

The coordination between the PIB here, their Information Offices at bases (Jammu, Pathankot, Sialkot etc) and the army PROs for the final lap was invariably absent. At every step, an ad-hoc situation was, it seemed, created and met, after much delay, tension and frustration on both sides. It seemed that nobody had any advance information about visiting Press parties, and only after they arrived was perhaps the first thought given to what was to be done.

The needs of newspapermen and more so of cameramen (TV and still) were never fully realized; the speed with which a news story (particularly a news story like this war) is to be covered, cleared and dispatched was not taken care of.

It was also felt that, at the Information base at the front, the national picture of the day should have been available. At least the day's handouts from Delhi could have been sent there by Teleprinter so that the correspondent at base could link his special story to the larger happenings of the day.

The priority given to correspondents to go to the front was often erratic and discriminatory. It could have been in some order, whatever the priorities were. It was felt that table thumping, daily visits to PIB, 'pushing' officials and 'contacts' with them helped. Some who just filed a written request (at the Government's instance) never heard anything further about it.

As mentioned earlier, censorship at front bases was slow, and correspondents were taken to 'safe' and 'quiet', sub-sectors of fronts. Some, who were around during the greatest tank battles, never saw one knocked – out enemy tank.

But as the experience was that once they reached the front the army commanders, right up to the General, were only too happy to receive them and talk to them frankly, often with brutal honesty and in confidence about tactics and operations. These were honoured by the correspondents and the whole treatment was a refreshing contrast to anything before or after the visit to the front. "The battle commanders and the Jawans proved to be better PR men, civilian or military".

At the Sikkim front a party had a four day pass and after an arduous and long journey by Jeep was given only one hour at the front to observe, or shoot pictures. Photographers were not allowed to shoot the faces of any officers or men.

Handouts

What was issued were not communiqués but statements giving the barest details. Every battle, skirmish or engagement was described in superlative terms. Whenever facts and figures of losses were given they should have been complete for both sides. It was bad psychology to keep quiet about our figures in one particular area or field and give only the enemy's. Handouts often referred to villages, rivers, bridges without explaining where they were, how far from major towns, what was their significance etc. Sometimes as the situation changed the names of the sectors were also changed, adding to confusion. The handouts cried out for briefing on the tactical side of the battles, which was not forthcoming.

It would appear that the handouts were written by knowledgeable Indian bureaucrats for knowledgeable bureaucrats and not for foreign correspondents, most of who were ignorant about basic facts about India.

The background material provided was inadequate and came in bits.

What would have made an immediate impact was if promptly on arrival, a man got quickly accredited (this was speedily done. in many cases but in some delayed because of petty points, like a picture not being the exact size, the clause which required you to state where we lived in the last five years etc. It was felt that peace time forms and queries were being used in an emergency situation), was given a kit containing a good map, background material, a list of do and don'ts, basic information about agencies and persons he would have to deal with etc.

General Observations

Everybody realized that too few people were doing too many things– "At base Information Centres one Information Officer was doing everything really, EVERYTHING".

But the general impression gathered was that there was no broad information policy evolved, no broad briefing given to those incharge of information the visiting reporters. If the Government wanted free and candid flow of information, everybody should have been told so (at PIB, Defence Ministry etc). The canons of military security, the broad objections of the Government should have been known to all those dealing with the Press. There appeared to be a complete mental block. Centralization of authority and responsibility led to a few men dealing with all problems and situations. The second or third level of officials were not able to dispose of anything at their level.

There should have been two distinct but coordinated wings – one to give information and the other to liaise with the Press and see that it gets to the news and the news gets to the papers.

Absence of this broad policy made everybody to keep pushing all the time – both officials and reporters.

Basic requirements like the need to feed the latest before deadlines for different parts of the world, concentration on agencies (including picture and TV) were not met.

The lack of coordination between the PIB and the Army was openly mentioned. It was particularly distressing to hear strangers talking of the 'little war' between the PIB and the Defence Wing, mentioning names of individuals concerned.

It is essential to give the impression that everything is under control and organized, even if it is not. This was not what happened.

A broad plan and an organization to implement is of Public Relations, Press coverage and facilities is essential to any big campaign today. Inspite of 1962, such a plan did not seem to have been drawn up by the Information Departments and the Army and everybody dealing with them felt that they were clueless and meeting every situation as it arose.

Here are some random but self-sufficient quotations.

"No one saw action" ..... "No one in the true sense covered the war"..... "We were never given any assurance about what the broad policy was, what to expect, when to expect and what to accept. So we kept on pushing, making things difficult for ourselves and for those who were helping us".... "I did not come half way round the world, at tremendous costs and rush to sit in New Delhi hotels and get a sun-tan in the swimming pools". "I have been covering the war for 20 years, have been in more defeats than victories, there are lulls during campaigns, but never have I covered the war without seeing any action". "Treat us with respect and confidence, let us feel that we are dealing with men who know their job and mind as well as ours and we shall not betray a confidence or not go along with your failings and inadequacies and not appreciate your difficulties or not be grateful for your facilities". "I was working in a vacuum". "I was told by your High Commission that as soon as I reach India, I shall be given accreditation and sent to the front. The first happened but I am still waiting for the second promise". "Your Public Relations and organization improved towards the end – but, alas, too late for any good to be done to us or to you".

Last Word

It was accepted that the visiting correspondents also did not do enough to help themselves. They should have joined the foreign correspondents association as temporary members and put in consolidated demands rather than individual. They could have been encouraged to do so.

Post Script

As an adjunct to the views collected from foreign and Indian correspondents a brief resume of the problems faced by the Government and of the basic difficulties can be attempted:

1. The PIB was taken somewhat unawares and, though it had an Emergency Unit, it was not enough to handle the situation. Many more people were needed. Some were indeed pulled out from elsewhere and pressed into service. Some Ministries weren't keen to have their Information Officers drafted for war service.
2. Extra staff was sanctioned, and money, but too slowly for needs.
3. There was imperfect sympathy and coordination between the Directorate of Public Relations (Defence) and the Press Information Bureau. This needs examination leading to possible reorganization.
4. Indian missions abroad could have been more careful before letting through so large a number of correspondents (those from Commonwealth countries didn't, however, need visas) and should not have given them a rosy picture of the facilities that would be available.
5. Correspondents are not always the most reasonable or cooperative of people. There are a number of instances of facilities being misused, of belligerency and discourtesy.
6. Regular censorship should probably have been set up. The Press Advising system may be adequate in peacetime but not in war. The Principal Information Officer's post and that of the Press Adviser should not have been left to one person. The PIO himself had been pressing for separation of the functions for quite some time.

   There was also the problem of handling dispatches in various foreign languages.

   Clearance was usually swift and not more than a handful of messages were withheld.
7. Communications between the PIB, the DPR (Defence), the base camps of the DPR and the fighting posts was imperfect.
8. The Army and its senior officers were conscious of security risks that might flow from the coverage of operations. Perhaps they erred on the side of over-caution but they had logic on their side.

The system of escorting correspondents was imperfect, that is probably why commanders appeared less co-operative than they, in fact, were.

9. The machinery for dealing with the correspondents began grinding slowly, but grew better.
10. The principle that Indian correspondents must have priority was generally accepted by all.
11. After some time the clearance of TV films by the Defence Attaches of the Indian embassies was adopted and worked well.
12. The spokesmen did not, at times; themselves know enough to be able to meet queries.

Appendix F

British Army Pre-deployment Training on Media

Do's

- Always be polite.
- Always report press present.
- Talk only about matters of fact within your area of responsibility.
- Refer all other questions to the PRO.
- Think before you speak.
- Try to be helpful.
- Be honest, positive, professional and remain calm.

Dont's

- Give any interviews without prior clearance from PRO.
- Discuss operations, plans and procedures.
- Give any information about local forces which might be of use to the opponents.
- Your thought and opinion are your own, never give them to media.
- Mislead or take sides.
- Let the media pressurise you into saying things you would never say or discuss.
- Carry the press in the vehicle unless authorised.

Source : Maj Gen Samay Ram (Retd), *Tackling Insurgency and Terrorism* (New Delhi: Manas , 2003), pp. 107-108.

Bibliography

Primary Sources

1. *From Surprise to Reckoning* : Kargil Review Committee Report (New Delhi: Govt. of India, Kargil Review Committee, 1999).
2. *Jammu and Kashmir Study Report* (New Delhi: USI, 2003).
3. Kargil Battle Diary of the author.
4. Minutes of ARTRAC Seminar on Media and National Security held at IIMC, New Delhi on 27-28 September 2000.
5. Interviews with numerous serving and retired officers of the three Services, media personalities, intellectuals and academicians.
6. *Pen and Sword*, Press Council of India Report, 1994.
7. Reforming the National Security System: Recommendations of Group of Ministers (GoM) – February 2001.

Secondary Sources

Books

1. Bajpai, Kanti, Afsir Karim and Amitabh Mattoo (eds), *Kargil and After: Challenges for Indian Police* (Delhi: Har-Anand Publications, 2001).
2. Bammi, YM, Lt Gen (Retd), *Kargil 1999: The Impregnable Conquered,* (NOIDA: Gorkha Publishers, 2002).
3. Baweja, Harinder, *A Soldier's Diary, : Kargil* (The *India Today* group, New Delhi: Books Today, 2000).
4. Bhatt, SC, *Media: Sensation not Truth* (New Delhi : Gyan Publishing House, 2003).
5. Dixit, JN, *India-Pakistan in War and Peace* (Delhi : Books Today, 2003).

6. Kanwal, Gurmeet, Col (Retd), *Heroes of Kargil,* an Army HQ Publication.

7. Kumar, Arvind, *Encyclopaedia of Mass Media and Communications*, Vol. IV (New Delhi : Anmol, 1998).

8. Matthews, Lloyd J, *Newsmen and National Defense: Is Conflict Inevitable?* (New York: Brassey's, 1991).

9. Morrison and Tumbler of 1988 on Journalism and War Reporting.

10. Mukherjee, Anjan, Col, *God of War: History of the Regiment of Artillery 1966-1999* (Directorate General of Artillery in association with Lancer's Publishers and Distributors, 2003).

11. Natarajan VC and Chakraborty AK, *Defence Reporting in India, The Communication Gap* (NOIDA : Trishul Publishers, 1995).

12. Parmar, Leena, *Armed Forces and the International Diversities* (Jaipur : Pointer Publishers, 2002).

13. Ram, Samay, Maj Gen (Retd), *Tackling Insurgency and Terrorism* (New Delhi : Manas, 2002).

14. Saxena, Sangeeta, *Defence Journalism in India* (New Delhi: Manas, 1997).

15. Singh, Amarinder, Capt (Retd), *A Ridge too Far : War in the Kargil Heights 1999,* (Patiala: Motibagh Palace, 2001).

16. Singh Harbakhsh, Lt Gen (Retd), *War Despatches: Indo-Pak Conflict 1965* (New Delhi : Lancer International, 1991).

17. Singh, Jasjit, Air Cmde (Retd) (ed), *Kargil 1999 : Pakistan's Fourth War for Kashmir* (New Delhi : Knowledge World, 1999).

18. Smith, Hedrick (ed), *The Media and the Gulf War – The Press and Democracy in Wartime,* (Washington D.C., Seven Locks Press, 1992).

19. Verma, A K, Maj Gen (Retd), *Kargil: Blood on the Snow* (Delhi: Manohar Publishers, 2002).

Articles, Papers and Periodicals

1. Bhattacharjea, Ajit, "The Nuke's Blunted Edge", *Outlook,* 5 July 1999.

2. Belknap, Margaret H, "The CNN Effect: Strategic Enabler or Operational Risk?", *Parameters* (Autumn 2002).

3. Bhatara, TK, Wg Cdr, "Media Management in the Services", *Defence Management* (November 1999 – April 2000).

4. Breakwell Glynis and Spacie Keith, "Pressures Facing Commanders", *The Occasional Paper* (No. 29, 1997), Strategic and Combat Studies Institute.

5. Chander, Subhash, Brig, "Info-War : Psychological Dimension", *NDC Papers 1/98*.

6. Chengappa, Raj, "Kargil War: Interview, Air Chief Marshal A Y Tipnis", *India Today*, 26 July 1999.

7. Cover Story, *Outlook Magazine*, 12 July 1999.

8. "Deterring Information Warfare: A New Strategic Challenge", *US Army War College Journal* (Winter 1996-1997).

9. Dixit, JN, "Field Marshal Cariappa Memorial Lecture 1997", *Sainik Samachar*, 1-15 March 1998.

10. Dreze, Jean, "Information, Democracy and the Military Establishment", *Vidura* (October-December 2002).

11. Ellinwood, Dr DeWitt C, "A Perspective on the Western Front by An Army Officer from India, Stand To", *The Journal of the Western Front Association* (January 2002).

12. Ganguly, Sumit, "Pakistan's Slide into Misery", *Foreign Affairs*, Vol. 81, No. 6 (November/December 2002).

13. Gokhale, Nitin A and Krishnan, Murali , "War and Witch Hunts", *Outlook*, 2 October 2000.

14. Gupta, VS, "Covering the War in Iraq", *Vidura* (April-June 2003).

15. Hakim, Rehana, "Media During Intense Conflict", *HIMAL* (June 2002).

16. Kant, Shruti, Col, "A Year After Kargil", *Sainik Samachar*, 1-15 October 2000.

17. Katyal, KK, Minutes of the Seminar on "Media and National Security", held at IIMC, New Delhi, 27-28 September 2000.

18. Kumar, Dinesh, "Soldiers and Scribblers- Media in Information Warfare: A Case Study of India", *Occasional Paper Series*, IDSA (June 2000).

19. Mattoo, Amitabh, "Mass Media in South Asia", *The Book Review*, Vol. XXVI, No. 1, January 2002.

20. Montogomery, DW, Brig, British Army, "Exploiting the Power of the Media", *NDC Papers 1/98*.

21. Nambiar, Satish, Lt Gen (Retd), "Reporting Comes of Age", *Vidura* (July-September 1999).

22. Noorani, AG, "The Defence Services and the Media", *Trishul*, Vol. IV, No. 2 (December 1991).

23. Natarajan, VC, "Media and Services – Need for More Interaction", *Trishul*, Vol. VI, No. 2 (January 1994).

24. *Newsweek Magazine*, 8 October 2001.

25. Prsanannan, R, "Gunslingers par Excellence", *The Week*, 20 February 2000.

26. Radhika V, Jathar DV and Routh Shiv Raj, *The Week*, 4 July 1999.

27. Raghavan, Jyoti, Book Review on *Media Ethics in Asia* (ed. Venkat Iyer), *Vidura*, (October-December 2002).

28. Rai, Ajai K, "Kargil Conflict and the Role of Indian Media", *Delhi Papers-17*, IDSA.

29. Rao, N Bhaskara, Dr, "Opportunities and Challenges", *Vidura* (January-March 2003).

30. Rao, N Bhaskara, *Indo-Pak Conflict, Controlled Mass Communication in Interstate Relations.*

31. Sachdev, AK, "Media Related Lessons from Kargil", *Strategic Analysis* (January 2000).

32. Sakhuja, SK, Col, "Media and Military-Some Lesser Appreciated Facts", *Combat Journal* (September 2001).

33. Sardeshpande, SC, Lt Gen (Retd), "Military and Media", *USI Journal*, Vol. 122, No. 510 (October – December 1992).

34. Singh, Daljeet Brig, "Information Warfare at the Strategic Level", *NDC Papers 3/97*.

35. Sinha, Dipankar, "Kargil Episode in Bengali Print Media", *Economic and Political Weekly*, 6 July 2002.

36. Sundarji, K, General (Retd), "Media and National Security", *Trishul*, Vol. IV, No.1 (July 1991).

37. Swami, Parveen, "War in Kargil", *Frontline,* 18 June 1999.

38. Swami, Praveen, in *Frontline*, 16 July 1999.

39. Swami, Ramesh Narayan, "National Information Policy", *NDC Papers 3/97*.

Newspapers

1. *The Asian Age*, Rahul Bedi, "Army Orders Investigation into Early Kargil Mistakes", 20 July 1999.

2. *The Asian Age* (New Delhi), 11 August 2000.

3. *The Herald* (Karachi), July 2000.

4. *The Hindustan Times*, Maj Gen Ashok K Mehta (Retd), "Kargil, Real and Imagined", 30 April 2000.

5. *The Hindustan Times*, Brahma Chellaney, "A New Myth Called Victory", 30 May 2000.

6. *The Indian Express,* General VP Malik (Retd), "Kargil : Where Defence Met Diplomacy", 25 July 2002.

7. *The Indian Express,* JG Nadkarni, "The Army Needs Modernisation", 11 August 1999.

8. *The Indian Express* (New Delhi), Rajdeep Sardesai, "Virtual Diplomacy; Don't Shoot the Messenger", *25* July 2001.

9. *The Kashmir Times*, "Kargil Martyrs: Uniting India", 26 July 2000.

10. *News* (Pakisatan), 25 July 1999.

11. *The Pioneer,* Gossly Unfair, editorial in 2001.

12. *The Pioneer*, Anil Bhat , "India's Costly Vijay at Kargil", 23 February 2002.

13. *The Pioneer,* M Divakar, "A Story That Refuses to Die", 10 August 2002.

14. *The Statesman* (New Delhi), "Tarnished Brass: Wither our Military Ethos?", 15 March 2002.

15. *The Times of India* , "Information as War" an editorial in April 28, 2000.

16. *The Times of India*, Siddhartha Varadarajan, "US Media Offer Sanitised Coverage", 12 October 2001.

17. *The Tribune,* Himmat Singh Gill, "Incisive Account of Indo-Pak Ties".

From the Net

1. Ivo Andric, "The Bridge on the Drina" (1945), downloaded from http://www.worldaffairsmonthly.com www.worldaffairsmonthly.com, on 24 March 2003.

2. JI Media Digest website.

3. May 2002, Conference Report on Kargil Project on www.ccc.nps.navy.mil

Index

Crygan